The Symmetries of September 11th

The Symmetries of September 11th

Ian Mordant

VANTAGE PRESS
New York

To my parents

Cover design by Susan Thomas

Published by Vantage Press, Inc.
516 West 34th Street, New York, New York 10001

Manufactured in the United States of America
ISBN: 0-533-14263-6

Library of Congress Catalog Card No.: 2002090508

0 9 8 7 6 5 4 3 2 1

"The bourgeoisie, wherever it has got the upper hand, has put an end to all feudal patriarchal, idyllic relations. It has pitilessly torn asunder the motley feudal ties that bound man to his 'natural superiors,' and has left remaining no other nexus between man and man than naked self-interest. . . . It has drowned the most heavenly ecstasies of religious fervour, of chivalrous enthusiasm, of philistine sentimentalism, in the icy water of egotistical calculation. . . . It has accomplished wonders far surpassing Egyptian pyramids, Roman aqueducts, and Gothic cathedrals. . . . The cheap prices of its commodities are the heavy artillery with which it batters down all Chinese walls, with which it forces the barbarians' intensely obstinate hatred of foreigners to capitulate. . . ."

—Karl Marx, Manifesto of 1848

"This book is not to be doubted."

—Very first verse of the Qur'an, i.e. Sura 2, Verse 1

Contents

Introductory Note to the Reader   ix
Acknowledgments   xi

I: The Symmetries of Everyday Life
  1. The Themes of This Book   3
  2. An Unusual Kind of Symmetry   8
  3. Each and Every Injustice Is a Symmetry   14
  4. A Further Kind of Symmetry   19
  5. Symmetries of Religion   22
  6. Symmetries versus Liberal Democracy   28

II: Symmetries versus Liberal Democracy
  7. Symmetries versus Liberal Democracy: The Case of Nazism   39
  8. Symmetries versus Liberal Democracies: The Thinking of
    Karl Marx   49
  9. Symmetries versus Liberal Democracy: The Case of
    the Middle East   54
 10. Other Symmetries of Political Life   82

III: The Economic Context of Terrorism
    Introduction   95
 11. What Liberal Capitalism Contributes to the World   97
 12. The Probability of Globalized Growth in
    Long-Term Destitution   111
 13. What the Next Unreliable Growth Phase Could Be Like   122

IV: Bringing the Pieces Together
 14. First Step to Fight Terrorism: A Use of Economic Boom   137

15. Second Step to Contain Terrorism: Terrorism, Democracy
    and Law   160
16. Democracy and the Future after September 11th   165

Bibliography   179

Introductory Note to the Reader

The struggle against terrorism does not follow neat boundaries and this book has, therefore, to pursue several themes. The first problem is to understand the motives and thinking of the attackers of September 11th and to realize that the central ideas of their thinking are clearly very attractive to some people. Why should this be so? There must be some theory of attractive falsities, and to discuss this, I have introduced a concept which will be new to most people. Accordingly, I chose to introduce it first in familiar situations, such as a marital quarrel and a divorce. Accordingly, chapters one through four deal with such situations; only then do I apply this understanding of attractive falsity to larger effects like those of religion, the Nazis, Communism and the highly unresolved situation between the Israelis and Palestinians.

I then go to observe that this kind of thinking, which can dominate political life, can be very dependent on economic context, so that chapters eleven through thirteen are about a particular aspect of economics that seems to me highly relevant to the struggle against terrorism. It is quite non-technical and no knowledge of economics is assumed. I then bring all these together in a final chapter, to leave the reader with a potential road to successful combating of terrorism for the future. I therefore recommend to the reader that this book is best read in the order in which the chapters are presented.

—Ian Mordant
email address: ianmordant@homechoice.co.uk

Acknowledgments

All authors owe vast debts to others, and I am no exception. The most obvious one in my case is my friend of twenty-five years standing, David Pavett. In all that time, I don't think a single week has gone by in which we haven't had a debate about something, often politics or philosophy. The book would have been much poorer without him.

A second large help has been another old friend, Rachel Benedyk, who has challenged my understanding and pointed out numerous gaps in my arguments. Eric Rayner has given me much encouragement over many years.

The author wishes to thank those who have kindly given their permission for the use of the illustrative material within this book:

The first six graphs of Chapter 12 of this book were drawn by the author from tables in *Long Waves of Capitalist Development*, Ernest Mandel, Second Revised Edition, Verso, 1995, and the tables have been used with the kind permission of Verso.

The final graph of Chapter 12 of this book is reproduced from Figure 4.3 in Rainer Metz (1992), *A Re-examination of Long Waves in Aggregate Production Series*, in Alfred Kleinknecht, Ernest Mandel and Immanuel Wallerstein's (eds) *New Findings in Long Wave Research*, New York: St. Martin's Press, ISBN 0333556542, pp. 80–119, and is reproduced with the permission of Palgrave Macmillan.

Finally, thanks to *The Independent* of London for permission to reprint on page 77 excerpts from a newspaper article by Michael Sheridan.

I
The Symmetries of Everyday Life

1

The Themes of This Book

Nothing leaves a person feeling more sore than unresolved injustice: the bitterness, the fury, the sense of outrage makes for pain and hurt of unbounded intensity. The pain and hurt would be unbounded in intensity, but unbounded in time, too, so that the hurting and other pains from an unresolved injustice can go on and on. The attacks in Washington and New York of September 11, 2001 were a good example of these aspects of injustice. Thus, had no attempt been made to pursue those who organized the attacks, the great mass of Americans would have been left with large hurting and pain, which would have continued without closure. It would have felt unbounded in intensity and in time.

Such painful emotions can be felt as quite unbounded, and that which is unbounded is infinite. It's the infinity of the pain that is the key problem. That's why unresolved injustice is problematic, why it is so warping, so destructive. America could not possibly turn the other cheek to the attacks of September, 2001, even if it had been sure that there would have been no further attacks. This question of infinity is the first theme of this book.

The last thing that infinities of pain guarantee is that their victims will attend to the cause of their pain in some rigorous carefully thought out way. We can easily see an extremely simple example of this added difficulty in our post-September 11 situation. Thus, consider the measures now being taken to try to prevent further instances of aircraft being used to crash into important buildings. We read of would-be passengers being much more intensively screened, of luggage being more carefully scrutinized, of all cutlery on board any jet aircraft being of plastic lest a metal knife, for instance, be used as a weapon to hijack the aircraft, the reinforcement of cabin doors to prevent unauthorized personnel entering the cockpit and so on. All these measures may indeed do something to reduce the number of hijackings of aircraft, but they will not prevent them, for a very simple reason. *Not a single one of these measures does anything to guarantee that the pilot and co-pilot of a jet aircraft are not Islamic or other religious militants who believe that death in the service of their cause will take them straight to heaven.* With all the thousands of people who pilot jet aircraft around the world, the probability that a handful will turn out to be political militants is, I suggest, a virtual certainty. There is excellent evidence from the past to expect this. We need only reflect on the fact that whilst each side in the Cold War set up intelligence services to spy on the other side, it was from right inside those very intelligence services that the greatest leaks to the other side occurred. Thus, the two men who most successfully spied *for* America and her allies were members of the Soviet intelligence service—Mr. Oleg Penkovsky and Mr. Gordievsky. Conversely, the man who was the most successful agent ever *for* the Soviet Union was a member of the British Secret Service, namely Mr. Kim Philby. Indeed, not merely was Kim Philby a member of British Intelligence, not merely did he combine this with being a Colonel in Soviet Intelligence, but he also managed for some seven years to combine this with being the very head of the Anti-Soviet Section of British Intelligence, in which role he also had to liaise with the very top people in American intelligence! Perhaps the Soviet Union's greatest penetration of the United States itself was via Mr. Aldrich Ames—whose official employer was none other than the Central Intelligence Agency. Reflecting on this history of political loyalties which occurred in the Cold War should help those who cannot imagine a pilot, who was employed for technical profi-

4

ciency in flying safely, could later turn out to be a political militant who deliberately destroys that aircraft. Those who are ignorant of their history are condemned to repeat it!

Yet, how can the development of such pilot-militants be prevented? How can any country's security service guarantee not merely that all current political intentions held by all pilots of its jet aircraft are peaceful ones, but that no such pilot will develop militant beliefs in the future? Note, it was the development of new militant attitudes amongst previously loyal staff that led to the assassination of the Prime Minister of India, Mrs. Indira Gandhi, in 1984. The two assassins were both of the Sikh faith, and had been recruited as security guards to the Prime Minister. At the time of their recruitment, they were apparently entirely loyal. But in 1984, the Prime Minister of India sent detachments of the Indian Army to violently dislodge religious militants who had taken control of one of the holiest shrines of the Sikh religion, namely the Golden Temple at Amritsar. It was a few months after the army had successfully stormed the militants in the Golden Temple that the Prime Minister was killed by two of her Sikh guards. Both guards had, it seems, been radicalized and, like the attackers of September 11, this was rooted in a feeling that their religion had been desecrated.

Some pilot of a jet aircraft in the future will very probably copy the attackers of September 11. Although some three thousand people were killed by the attacks of September 11, the damage to America could have been much much greater. It will be one aim of this book to argue that great damage to the economy of America would be disastrous for the rest of the world, including the fifty-odd countries of the world in which Muslims are in the large majority. It is this last point which will be vital to get across if the results of future terrorist attacks are not to be disastrous for the world. *A successful struggle against terrorism, more than anything else, requires careful economic and political thought.* Po-

5

licemen and soldiers have a role to play in the struggle against terrorism as they did in Afghanistan in the months immediately after September 11, but a successful struggle long-term against terrorism will make it a small role.

September 11, 2001 was not the first date on which America discovered its security was not as great as it had thought. On October 4, 1957, the then Soviet Union launched its first spacecraft, Sputnik 1, and Americans and others in the advanced capitalist countries shuddered at the possibility that the Soviets would be able to rain atomic bombs down on them from outer space. Plainly, the Soviets had stolen a march on the Americans just as Mr. Bin Laden succeeded in doing in the run-up to September 11. The fears after the attacks of September 11 have some resemblance to the fears after that day in 1957, and the two situations have some similarities and some differences. I will use both of these to provide some thought about our new post-September 11th world.

This book is written on the assumption that unless we can intervene successfully, future terrorist attacks will cause much greater devastation than that of September 11. This would be because just as those fighting terrorism have learned from September 11th, so, in all likelihood, have the terrorists as well. We can see an everyday example of this dialectic at work. Those who write software to counteract the effects of viruses that are sent over the internet become better and better at it, but so too do the authors of these viruses. After some fifteen years, those who produce anti-virus software have not so far found a way of cumulatively reducing the number of viruses around, the damage they can do, etc., despite having every current mathematical and computer software sophistication to call on. For one thing, the writers of the viruses enjoy the advantage of surprise, as did the attackers of September 11th. As I remarked at the beginning of this section, success against terrorism will require an unusual rigor of thinking; it will require indeed that opponents of terrorism do better than the writers of anti-virus software. One aim of this book is to help show what this involves.

I began with the unboundedness or infinity of the feelings and perceptions of those who carried out the attacks of September 11th, as well as of Americans who feel themselves attacked. In my next four chapters, I will develop a way to think about this, and help to prevent thinking itself to be overwhelmed by the infinities of pain that derive from perceptions of injustice.

2

An Unusual Kind of Symmetry

Many years ago, someone with schizophrenia said to me, "We have a Siamese cat at home. He is thinking of me." Evidently this man had been thinking of the family's cat, but in his head, "I am thinking of the cat" had become "he is thinking of me." He had reversed the subject and the object. In "I am thinking of the cat," the man is the subject and the cat is the object, whereas in "he is thinking of me," the cat is the subject, and the man is the object.

For the man to reverse subject and object in this way is for him to treat both "I am thinking of the cat" and "he is thinking of me" as interchangeable. This is something which can happen in the thinking of schizophrenics—it allowed this man to treat as interchangeable, two sentences that non-schizophrenics would not normally interchange.

But *how* might this form of thought structure occur? Well, if "thinking" was operating purely *abstractly* for this man, that is to say if his own idea of "thinking" was sufficiently abstracted from whether a cat or a human was doing the thinking, then he could interchange "I am thinking of the cat" with "he is thinking of me." In this way, "I am thinking of the cat" and "he is thinking of me," would attain a degree of equivalence.

To treat two things the same in this way is to treat them symmetrically, but a very misleading kind of symmetry. That was why a psychologist by the name of Matte Blanco invented the term *symmetrization.* It is a kind of absurd equating, treating as symmetrical, two things which someone whose thinking was not so sensationally abstract would not do. This was what the man described above could engage in: because his perception of "thinking" could at some moment be very abstract, he could, at that moment, abstract away from the many actual differences between two things, namely his own thinking and that of his cat. As a result, he could, on that occasion, treat two different things which had lots of differences as the same. This is what Blanco would call "symmetrizing" the two things.

I'll take a second instance of symmetrization in which I will quote a case quoted by Matte Blanco. This involved another man, also with schizophrenia, who had consulted his dentist after being bitten by a dog. Why did he do this? If that man had thought only of "bad teeth" and thought about them *sufficiently abstractly,* he could treat the dog's teeth and the man's teeth as interchangeable. So "bad teeth" tacitly became his own teeth, and this then had led him to visit the dentist. Again, the odd outcome was from a style of thinking that was amazingly abstract. If one did think that abstractly, the interchangeability of man's teeth and the dog's teeth could occur. This was the same pattern as with the cat's thoughts of the previous example. (Matt Blanco 1975, p. 317)

I'll take just one further example from people with schizophrenia. A man faced with the sound of a siren from a police car passing his home had rushed from the chair in which he was sitting, and put his head into the freezer. Asked why he had done this, he replied: "Because I don't want the cops to hear my thoughts on their police radios." Asked how putting his head in the freezer stopped the police from hearing his thoughts, he had replied, "Frozen things can't move, so by freezing my thoughts, they weren't able to run to where the cops are trying to listen in."

I reflect that this man knew that his brain produced waves, and that a radio picks up waves. So, if at that moment "waves" was a completely abstract term for this man, then in his understanding his brain waves and the waves that enter a radio would be interchangeable. In that case, what indeed was there to stop the police listening in to them? To maintain his privacy, it could thereby seem to this man that he would have to stop his brain waves from moving. The action of "moving" must also be very abstract for him, and he understood that nothing which is frozen can move. Therefore, putting his head in the freezer would indeed seem to him to be a way to freeze the waves from his brain, and so stop them from moving to where the police had their radios.

In each case, he treated two different things, such as two kinds of waves (those of his brain and those which enter police radios), as sufficiently similar as to be interchangeable. By contrast, someone without schizophrenia would not generally do this.

This symmetrization is not itself to be confused with, say, the symmetry of two halves of a circle. These are simply identical. Symmetrization arises when the degree of abstraction leaves behind many of the central qualities of two different things. When such abstraction is made from two different things, they can come to be inaccurately perceived as mainly similar, when in fact in reality they have large and crucial differences.

Therefore, crucial to schizophrenic thinking is its immense abstraction. In the thought of a schizophrenic, nouns like "teeth" or verbs like "thinking" operate in abstraction from any mouth that contained those teeth or any particular sentient entity that actually engaged in thought.

A Second Type of Symmetrization

The examples of symmetrization mentioned so far did not produce any extreme feelings . . . of the kind of intense pain and hurt experienced at the perception of injustice. By contrast, consider Stan and Donna, who are having a marital quarrel when she turns on him and shouts, "You bastard!" Now, he does of course have his "bastardy" parts, but at that moment, for her, he is *all* bastard, *only* bastard, *wholly* bastard. This, too, is a kind of symmetrization, namely one which equates the whole of that husband with a bastardy part, so that in such moments the whole person is perceived as a bastard. In that moment, her anger towards him can readily feel unbounded, or infinite. Also it has occurred because, at that moment, she perceived him as having just one attribute—bastard. He, therefore, had to be *all* bastard, *only* bastard.

This outcome, where a single attribute produces perceptions of unboundedness, is common. Thus, take the blackness of the night; there is only blackness, complete blackness and it feels completely unbounded. As before, whatever is unbounded is infinite. There is the complete absence of the perception of any limit.

We may readily see another example of this process. On her wedding day, a bride in a Christian wedding may be dressed all in white, and her bridesmaids are dressed all in white, and this creates an image of unbounded purity: as it's meant to. Again, any single attribute will have this effect of unboundedness, or infinity.

Now, this outcome of infinity is what can readily occur when some perceived whole is equated with just some of its essential attributes, losing all others. That's why the symmetrization between that whole and that part has a special name, namely a *whole-part symmetrization*. This is my second type of symmetrization, with which the title of this section began. It is this type of equating that tends to produce an infinity. I will demonstrate this as follows.

Demonstration

Firstly, I can be sure that I have as many fingers on my left hand as on my right hand if I let the tip of each finger on the left hand touch the tip of the corresponding finger on the right: the tip of my left thumb touches the tip of my right thumb, the tip of my left forefinger touches the tip of my right forefinger, and so on.

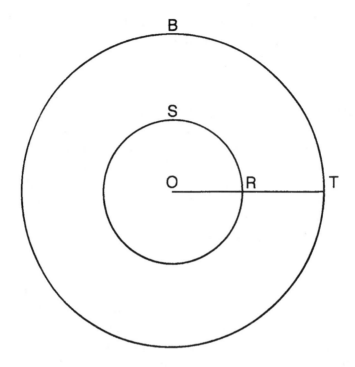

Each tip on my left touches just one tip on my right, each tip on my right touches exactly one tip on my left.

Now, imagine that I have two circles. I have a small circle, *S*, and a big circle, *B*. Each circle is drawn on the same center, O. Mathematically, each single point on the circle has no thickness, so that there are an unbounded number of such points on any circle.

I chose the circumference of circle S to be half the circumference of circle B. We could thus lay this distance S on half the distance B. As S is half as long as B, S might be thought to have half as many points as B. Does it?

One answer to this question is to proceed to pair off each point on S with a point on B. This can be done with a line. Start from O and the line cuts the small circle at R and the big circle at T.

Now a line also has no thickness, so it touches just one point on the small circle and just one point on the big circle.

Now reverse the operation of the line. Start at T on the big circle and go in to the center O. The line cuts the small circle exactly once at R.

What we have on the two circles is like the fingers on the two hands. Each point, R, on the small circle goes to just one point, T, on the large circle, and each point, T, on the large circle goes to the same point R on the small circle. We have thus paired off each point on the small circle with exactly one point on the big circle, just as we paired off each finger on one hand with one finger on the other. Just as the result was that we had as many fingers on each hand, our latest conclusion is that each circle now has as many points as the other.

So S is half as long as B—yet S has as many points as B!

This can't happen with just a finite number, like five, it's the sort of thing that can only happen with an unbounded, limitless, number of points. So, we see how, when you equate a circle with one half its size, this produces an unboundedness, that is, an infinity.

In my next chapter, I will argue that each and every injustice is caused by a whole-part symmetrization.

3

Each and Every Injustice Is a Symmetry

We saw in the previous chapter how an unbounded feeling of anger or loathing may occur in, say, a marital quarrel, and that it can come about by what I called a whole-part symmetrization. Now, I am going to argue that the perception of injustice derives from the perception of a whole-part symmetrization, and such symmetrization also produces the associated notorious fury and rage in the recipient. My examples in this section are taken from private life.

I'll start with a divorce. Stan and Donna are getting divorced, and must thus share out their joint assets from the marriage. Donna thinks that Stan is claiming more than his fair share. As a result, he is tacitly allocating to her a smaller amount than she thinks fair. Thus, Donna implicitly thinks that Stan is equating what she thinks is fair to her, to some smaller amount. That, she feels, is his injustice to her. From his side, Stan is similarly indignant at Donna's claim, since as this is bigger than he thinks she deserves, this means that what he takes to be his fair share is thereby being equated to some smaller amount. Each person takes the other's claim of justice to be unjust, and the nature of this injustice is the equating of some whole amount of money to one of its parts. Each party is livid to hear the other person call their proposals just; indeed that the other person can call so manifestly an unfair settlement fair just proves what a two-faced double-dealing bastard the other person is finally revealed to be! As I observed, each person tacitly takes the other person's very act of injustice to consist of a whole-part symmetrization.

I also note the completely disproportionate hatred and fury which people in such a situation feel towards each other. The utter unboundedness of these feelings is, for them, an infinity. A bitterly fought-over divorce is a case of where the perception of an injustice is an overwhelming source of psychic pain, of bitterness and resentment, because each person feels that they are on the receiving end of someone else's whole-part symmetrization.

I'll now give a second illustration of my link between injustice and whole-part symmetrization. A man is attacked by another man armed with an axe and bent on robbery, and in the course of the attack, the victim loses an arm. He has evidently thereby been done a large injustice, given that the attack has left him with a number of permanent disadvantages, physical, psychological and aesthetic. So, where is the whole-part symmetrization in all this?

To answer this, I would compare the attacked man before the robbery and after. His self (whole) before the robbery has been forcibly equated to his self (less whole) after the robbery. That is the injustice that the attacker has done him. There might also be further whole-part symmetrizations; for instance the everyday feelings of security that that person needs to go about daily life had also now been equated to zero. This latter symmetrization produces a further injustice to the attacked man.

We may contrast all this with the situation of a person born with only one arm and he still therefore only has one arm. In this latter situation, we would be much more likely to have said that he was disadvantaged. To be disadvantaged is not the same as suffering an injustice, in that the cause did not involve a malignant intention. The two situations would have some consequences in common, such as various forms of pain. But the instance of disadvantage shows that not all painful outcomes can be traced to injustice.

My third example goes like this: a young girl is sitting on a bus, and on the empty seat next to her she builds an imaginary home. Her father, looking for somewhere to sit, comes and sits next to his child. Isn't she devastated! The beautiful home she had built in her imagination on the seat is completely destroyed! Her fury at Daddy knows no bound . . . is boundless, and whatever is boundless is infinite. She feels that he has done her and her friends in the house an injustice! It derives from a perceived symmetrization, in this case that her beautiful imaginary home has been destroyed. Any destruction is a symmetrization, because the thing destroyed is equated to zero. Equating to zero is always possible since we know from the mathematics of set theory that everything has a zero part.

Here, we have three examples of injustice, and in each case the person who felt that they had suffered the injustice felt that they had received it from some other person.

There is, however, another kind of injustice namely the kind a person can feel guilty about having done to someone else. Take an example of a man who was rude to his father hours before that father died. The guilt a person can feel from such an occurrence can be quite unbounded . . . that is, infinite. It can also go on timelessly for decades, and so be unbounded in practice in time as well. People who we call depressed regularly manifest such infinities of emotional intensity and they can continue for year after year after year. But how, on the understanding of injustice as a whole-part symmetrization, can one do an injustice to oneself?

Again, I'll mention someone I once knew. He had known for some twenty years before he finally went blind that this was going to happen. When I asked him about this, he told me that when he was told about the coming blindness, he had just cut off the matter from his body, that since then he had had no feelings towards it. This is surely a whole-part symmetrization, where his feelings for his body were equated to having no feelings for it.

If I ask where the injustice here was, I would firstly say that it's one's body which keeps one alive. Not to have feelings towards one's own body, and good feelings indeed, is already an injustice to one's own sense of self, to one's feeling of self-worth. Those valuable good feelings were equated by this man to no feelings, but I also think it helped him commit further injustices to himself. Thus, in the many years that his sight was failing, but still fairly good, he made no serious effort to acquire any skill; indeed, he did not even try to learn Braille. So, he was committing a massive injustice to himself in leaving himself quite unable to earn a living when he would be at his most handicapped. Had he allowed himself to go on having feelings towards his body, he might well have been sufficiently motivated to think about his future.

As the skill he could have acquired before going blind was not acquired, so the potential that he had to acquire it was equated to zero too; it was symmetrized out. Here was another injustice-creating symmetrization.

Certainly, when I listened to him talk, I think he had tacitly equated all his abilities to his ability to see, so that all his abilities became degenerative. Via this symmetrization, he felt that to develop, say, his skill in computing was about as sensible as trying to become a skilled microscopist. Via this symmetrization, he did himself a major injustice, and it produced infinities, such as his unending despair.

Note that such perceptions of injustice can readily go on indefinitely; they do not always diminish over time. This deserves a paragraph on its own. Generally, time is a wholly sequential process, so that today is always, but always before tomorrow. But if symmetrization is in charge, it could symmetrize out this sequential aspect of time, and so it would feel as though the injustice only happened very recently, hence people can smart under the perception of injustice not just for an hour or two or a week or so, but still feel the pain years and decades after the injustice was done. The symmetrization that produced that perception of injustice, and produced its pain, has also symmetrized out the passing of time.

I would summarize all this as follows: The perception of injustice is actually the perception of a moral symmetrization. Infinities of pain surround the perception of injustice, because both the injustice and the pain are each produced by the self-same symmetrization. No wonder that people involved in divorce can be bursting with fury at each other's claim! No wonder constructive discussion between divorcing couples seems to often disappear. Yet, if there are children involved, they are likely to have to stay in touch—frequently across unresolved infinities of disdain, loathing and the like. Timelessness can be seen to operate if, years later, neither can refer to the other except through clenched teeth. The anger at whichever injustice is being perceived hasn't diminished over time.

So, the perception of injustice produces pain which can feel unbounded in intensity and go on and on and on. No wonder the perception of injustice causes so much trouble!

4

A Further Kind of Symmetry

I will now introduce a type of symmetrization that I think is central to the belief system of those who give their lives for what they take to be a Divine cause, as did the attackers of September 11th. I will introduce my discussion of their symmetry via an example from a clinical scenario: the syndrome of depression.

Characteristically, the depressive person has perceptions that are in some crucial ways *completely different, wholly different, purely different* from everyone else, and that consciously, at least, that difference is wholly negative. As far as the depressed person is consciously concerned, nobody is as bad, or nobody is as ugly, or nobody is as unworthy of love and respect as she or he is. The depressive perceptions are that she or he differs from everyone else, and the differences all cast the depressed person in a bad light. Thus, in what is generally called depression, *all* of a person's attributes are equated to only *some* of their attributes, namely the person's perceived failings. Strikingly, the feelings that make up depression generally feel completely unbounded in their intensity and in time; that is to say the person feels as though they will always be as valueless as they now feel. They feel utterly dreadful and it seems that such feelings will go on for ever; there is infinity of intensity of (bad) feeling and a perceived infinity of time. That's why some depressives kill themselves. They can see no other way out of the utterly black tunnel in which they believe they are doomed to be.

19

So depression is about infinity and it's an infinity which results from the person's perceived loss of similarities with others. This is therefore a *symmetrization,* but it's a different kind from those I have so far written about. Since it's an infinity that results from a perceived loss of similarity, I will call this type of symmetrization the *difference infinity*; it reflects the emphasis on difference, predominant difference, overwhelming difference.

How does such a difference infinity arise? How does the depressive person, for instance, lose their perception of sharing the good attributes of others? My answer is that this type of symmetrization is also an outcome of *abstraction*: people lose their perceptions of similarity because they abstract from these. As before, a whole is thereby equated to one of its parts, except that in this case the conscious equating is to a bad part, and the result is that those bad parts feel unboundedly bad. That is why those bad parts feel so dominant.

Nor is this all. Since injustice is produced by whole-part symmetrization, it comes as no surprise to me to observe that depressed people are often deeply unjust, at least emotionally, both to themselves and to their intimate relationships. What makes the treatment of depression so difficult is that the depressed person would instantly agree that they are being unjust! However, what is unjust is not the existence of that person—as the depressed person would feel—but the operation of the difference infinity, which is what both produces and maintains that depression.

We can also observe the importance of abstraction in relation to depression in another way. People who suffer from depression tend to want to stay in bed. On the one hand, bed can feel warm, holding, loving and giving, all the things people with depression so want, but are in despair at ever getting, or deserving to get. Bed feels like the nearest thing to getting those things. That's one reason that badly depressed people stay in bed. But bed isn't really any of those holding, loving, giving things: bed is actually a site of abstraction. Yes, bed does lend itself to feeling a kind of warmth, but it is not the warmth of love at all. To be loving and loved is to experience acceptance by another person; by contrast, to lie in bed by oneself is the very opposite. By means of abstraction, that bed can feel as if it is capable of giving some warmth and accepting the way a loving partner or spouse would do. Lying in bed is very seductive for someone with depression, but like all seduction, it is ultimately destructive to the person who is seduced.

This in turn raises the question as to whether there is a link between infinity and seduction, and I think that there is a very strong link indeed. For it seems to me that it is infinity itself that is always the seductive attribute. For example, sexual seduction occurs through a fantasy that the pleasure of an offer will be entirely boundless, and infinitely satisfying.

Sexual seduction is a highly pleasant fantasy, but others are much less so. Take the apparent universality of enjoyment of envy; this is a seduction by an extremely unpleasant infinity, the infinity of destructiveness. I suspect that it is from this that arose the basic Christian teaching that man is inherently evil. After all, evil is evidently an infinity, for it has no bound on it. Also, the doing of so-called evil is deeply attractive, as religious thinkers have noted down the centuries, and struggled with, and whose origin they have tried to understand via their construct of Satan. Satan, indeed, is a collection of infinities, all of them negative. The truth, I suggest, is that it is infinity that is seductive.

I will now look at other instances of the difference infinity.

5

Symmetries of Religion

The attackers of September 11th were undoubtedly believers in one intentional Creator of the universe. Judaism, Christianity and Islam all imply that their deity is omnipotent, omniscient and infinitely just, or loving, in the Christian case. Let's apply the ideas of the previous four chapters here. The first idea is that the attributes of each deity are infinities: omnipotence has no limit, and so this potency, being unbounded, is infinite. Then, there is omniscience, which means no limit on what the deity can know, and so this, too, is infinite. Finally, to be infinitely just or loving is just that. So, these attributes are clearly infinite in amount.

A second point is that the deities of Judaism, Christianity or Islam only have good attributes. All other sentient beings have both good and bad attributes, but God by contrast is wholly different in this matter, the most perfect difference from anything else imaginable. The deity of Judaism, Christianity and Islam is thus an excellent example of the difference infinity. Indeed, the deity God seems to be the most perfect possible example of a difference infinity.

A third point is that the details of the attributes of God are timeless; that is, they are unchanging in time. They are, therefore, infinite in time as well.

All this is exactly what you would expect if the attributes of God were abstracted from whatever obstructs their total operation. It is this abstraction, I say, which constructs the difference infinity, and which produces these infinities. The particular symmetrization is evidently the one that results from God having only good attributes: all possible attributes are equated to just positive ones. That is why none of them act as bound to any others; only an attribute which was negative, or inadequate in some way, could be such a bound.

So, God is constructed from abstracted good attributes only, and accordingly, God doesn't bear any resemblance to anything anyone has seen or can describe. God is thus pure difference, but where the depressive is at negative infinities, God is at the opposite pole, towering and stretching far above you, apparently magnificently good and triumphant in every way. This outcome helps maintain belief in the abstraction that is God.

The use of infinities in religion also covers the concepts of heaven and hell, two infinities representing very different fates experienced. So, what we have here is a pair of infinities, and a pair that define themselves by their differences from each other. I conclude that what we have is a pair of difference infinities. I shall have occasion to come back to such pairs quite frequently in later chapters.

These perspectives of God seem to be easily observable in the holy book of Islam, namely the Qur'an. I especially mention the Qur'an partly because the attackers of September 11th were believers in the Qur'an. The Qur'an is distinguished from other holy books in that it is supposed to be transcribed by just one man, namely Mohammed. Other holy books contain transcriptions from many people, and that makes for all manner of differences between these different people. These problems of differences in different transcribers are absent from the Qur'an.

In the Qur'an, we can readily see claims about the timeless infinite goodness of the attributes of God. For example, I'll take just three such verses, (which I have found in reading a version of the Qur'an which has been rendered into English by Mr. N.J. Dawood, Penguin Classics, 1998). In this rendering, Chapter or Sura 23 verse 1, reads:

> Blessed are the believers who are humble in their prayers; who avoid profane talk and give alms to the destitute; who restrain their carnal desires (except with their wives and slave-girls, for these are lawful to them: transgressors are those who lust after other than these); who are true to their trusts and promises, diligent in their prayers. These are the heirs of Paradise; they shall abide in it forever.

Then there is Mr. Dawood's rendering of Chapter or Sura 4, Verse 34:

> Men have authority over women because God made the one superior to the other, and because they spend their wealth to maintain them. Good women are obedient. They guard their unseen parts because God has guarded them. As for those from whom you fear disobedience, admonish them and forsake them in beds apart, and beat them. Then, if they obey you, take no further action against them. Surely God is high, supreme.

Then there is Mr. Dawood's rendering of Chapter or Sura 5, Verses 33 to 35:

> Those that make war against God and His apostle and spread disorder in the land shall be slain or crucified or have their hands or feet cut off on alternate sides or be banished from the land. They shall be held up to shame in this world, and in the world to come grievous punishment awaits them: except those that repent before you reduce them. For you must know that God is forgiving and merciful.

One thing that immediately catches the eye of any student of symmetrization is how each of the three verses ends with an infinity of some kind, whether of paradise, or of God who is said to be high and supreme, or being forgiving and merciful. But the morality of the verses is, at least in part, utterly at variance with what is taken to be justice in a liberal context. When the details are examined, it's fairly easy to conclude that this situation has arisen because the beliefs expressed in the verses are abstractions from what was normal and everyday at the time the Qur'an was assembled. For instance, the idea from our first quote that it is just for a slave owner to sexually take a slave girl is surely an abstraction from the morality which existed when the Qur'an was being assembled. At that time, some of the women taken into slavery were from tribes whom the Muslims had conquered, and enslaving these women was less unjust than killing them. In the context of that choice, the provisions of the verse in respect of slave-girls is plainly an abstraction from this less unjust choice, but to treat the morality of the verse as something that can't be improved on because it is in the Qur'an is a symmetrization. This is because it is treating a moral precept that had some just application at *one* time as if it had total just application for *all* time. *All* time is being equated to *some* time; this is a whole-part symmetrization and it produces the fantasy that the provisions of the verse are infinitely just, and for all time.

I claimed earlier that it is infinity that is seductive. So, because the infinities of God are only good ones, they are bound to be seductive unless obstructed by objections rigorous enough not to be readily denied. This can only happen when a whole culture moves against belief in the infinities of God, and because that has happened most strongly in Europe, it is there that one sees the greatest cries of anguish at the "death of God," i.e. the infinities of Christianity have increasingly become less believable.*

Of course, once the idea that the deity of the holy books exists through a kind of abstraction is accepted, then some things that puzzle people about religion become promptly understandable. For example, there is firstly the fact that many people have engaged in acts of killing as a result of their commitments to their religion. If religious beliefs are fantasized abstractions, then the ability to abstract from the suffering of those you kill and harm can become easy. But even more interesting, especially perhaps since September 11th, is the failure of the religious authorities to try and tackle the terrorists who issue from their own religious tradition. For example, in Northern Ireland, there are terrorists from both the Roman Catholic and Protestant communities. Now, I have yet to hear of any ongoing, thought-out, consciously intended programme from either side of the religious divide that actually tackles and challenges the convictions of the terrorists from their tradition.

So, to sum up, terrorists are people for whom the infinity of religious conviction has proved utterly seductive; who wish to reach the infinity of God's reward through their actions; and who make abstraction from the suffering by individuals. Religious abstraction can thus be a large excuse.

Judaism and Islam have the equivalent problem in that their

---

*The writer A.N. Wilson has a deeply interesting book on the subject, *God's Funeral* (John Murray, London, 1999). His blurb sums up by saying how, "The decline in religious certainty . . . brought on a devastating sense of emotional loss which extends to our own times." That "devastating" is surely experienced as boundless, and thus an infinity. A Christian Priest, Rev. Rodney Bomford, has a book, *The Symmetry of God,* (Free Association Press, London and New York, 1999) which tries to think about symmetrization and Christian belief. But he approaches this question as a theologian, rather than in the way done here.

men of the cloth have not rushed to call for terrorists from their own side to be hunted down and imprisoned. As long ago as 1948, terrorists from the Jewish side murdered some 200 Arab civilians (at Deir Yassin) and three days later, Arab terrorists killed some ninety-seven Jewish civilians (who were on their way to the Hadassah Hospital in marked Red Cross vans). Over fifty years later, I have yet to come across any man of either cloth who has called for the imprisonment for life of the terrorists who had issued from their respective religious beliefs. The two religious authorities have not even tried to change the attitudes of those who have been convicted of terrorism. Had convicted terrorists renounced their old motivations for the terrorist crimes they had committed, this would have seriously reduced recruitment of new volunteers to the terror organizations, such as the Jewish Irgun terrorist group or the Islamic Hamas terrorist group. So there is a striking lack of morality at the religious organizational level, or so it seems to me. This could have some important consequences in the Middle East; for instance two of Israel's prime ministers, namely Menachem Begin and Yitzchak Shamir, and the Palestinians' Yassir Arafat all came to office as ex-terrorists. Perhaps, had they been made to confront their terrorist pasts, their later political behavior would have been less obstructive to settlement and cooperation.

All in all, we see how lamentable have been the responses of all three monotheisms to combating terrorists from within their own communities. If the deity with whom they are concerned is an outcome of abstraction, this is not surprising.

6

Symmetries versus Liberal Democracy

Take two democratic ideas: that of choosing governments by means of one adult/one vote elections, and that of open public criticism and dissent. At first glance, these might not seem to have much to do with each other, but I think that they necessarily have a great deal to do with each other, and I think that we can see this as follows. Only if there is open criticism of all matters of public policy and of morality and of the laws that exist, or fail to exist, is the method of choosing governments by election authentic; only then does it have any chance of not being an act of manipulation. Conversely, if there is a multi-party one adult/one vote system of government, the restriction of those criticisms permitted in public becomes much more difficult, although such restrictions may be possible. In short, conditions of liberal democracy are those in which the preservation of infinities that derive from symmetrization are most easily exposed as being just that, and a process of de-infinitization can occur. Thus, amidst all the fashionable cries about the 'death of god' within Christianity, especially, it has become difficult for potential terrorists from within Christianity, one of the religions most affected so far by liberal democracy, to summon up a divine excuse for acts of terrorism. Militants who bomb abortion clinics in the United States are the most frequent examples of terrorists from within Christianity, yet they evidently enjoy little support even within the wide swathe of American fundamentalist Christians who wholly oppose abortion.

Terrorists from within the Jews who live in the West Bank and Gaza Strip have a little more acceptance amongst Israelis than the abortion clinic bombers have amongst Christians, but not that much more. Thus, Baruch Goldstein, the Jewish-Israeli terrorist who killed twenty-nine Muslim worshippers in a mosque in Hebron, has had no imitators amongst the Jews, who almost universally condemn his action. The African National Congress of South Africa supported armed struggle against the apartheid regime for thirty years, 1960–1990, but engaged in very, very few attacks on white civilians. The Irish Republican Army enjoyed negligible support in the Irish Republic for whom they held themselves to be fighting: whenever they have stood for election in the Republic, Sinn Fein, the IRA's political wing, turned in derisory percentages: like two percent of the vote, and that was in a constituency for which it chose to fight! It tried to substitute terrorism for democracy but failed due to the dominant democratic political culture in Britain, Northern Ireland, and the Irish Republic.

By contrast, terrorism from within Muslim communities has had less opposition, and I submit that this is primarily because those countries where Muslims were the large majority of the population tend to operate with an inadequate amount of open, liberal, democratic dissent. I will illustrate my belief by recalling Mr. Dawood's rendering of Sura 23, verse 1 from the Qur'an into English:

> Blessed are the believers who are humble in their prayers; who avoid profane talk and give alms to the destitute; who restrain their carnal desires (except with their wives and slave-girls, for these are lawful to them: transgressors are those who lust after other than these); who are true to their trusts and promises, diligent in their prayers. These are the heirs of Paradise; they shall abide in it forever.

This could be taken as a license for barbarism, as follows:

First Example of Barbarism

A man can have sex with a woman to whom he is not married, namely with a slave-girl, but this is evidently not adultery, for she is "lawful" to a believer, from which I conclude that the slave-girl is not considered a human being, since were a Muslim man to have sex with a human female who was not a slave and to whom he was not married, it would be adultery. Therefore, the meaning of the verse uses slavery to dehumanize the person.

Second Example of Barbarism

The verse is also capable of licensing racism since many a slave in Muslim society was black, having come from the East African coast (which is strongly Islamic to this day as a result of the attentions of the Muslim slave trade). So, the slave-girl might well be of another race, so to license sex with her, irrespective of her will, would be racist, too.

This (rather Western) interpretation of the Qur'an can be openly expressed in Europe, but in few countries where Islam is the dominant religion could one assert this in a newspaper or via radio or television. My conclusions about that verse may be open to a challenge, but this is not my main point. My point is the difficulty I, or anyone else, would encounter in expressing these conclusions in public media in most countries where Islam is the dominant religion. It is this pre-liberal-democratic, political situation which I think maintains ignorant, or evasive, symmetrizations. This is one reason why terrorists from Muslim society show signs of encountering fewer constraints on the formation of their terrorist intentions, because these derive from infinities of hate, for which religion can be so notable a source.

Democracy can, in fact, crush terrorism. Here is an example: the way in which Israel's elected Prime Minister, David Ben

Gurion, defeated the organizations of Jewish terrorism, after the Israeli state came into existence in 1948, by gathering public support through Israel's democratic traditions and process. I will go into more of the particular details of this in my chapter on the Middle East.

All this runs parallel to another consideration. We saw earlier that the perception of injustice is always the outcome of a symmetrization, so if that symmetrization is one that exists due to ignorance or evasion, then we would have the perception of injustice that was due to ignorance or evasiveness. If, as is likely, the attackers of September 11th believed the United States to be the "Great Satan" and the Great Satan is evidently unboundedly bad . . . infinitely bad . . . then we have the example of a fantasized infinity, familiar to any student of symmetrization. The fantasist believes that the effects of the United States are *all* bad, all destructive, of say Arabs and Muslims, instead of being able to say that the United States has *some* destructive effects, and some constructive ones, too, such as perhaps having done the most to develop drugs that inhibit the development of AIDS.

Apart from their beliefs about America, up to September 11th the attackers behaved normally, sufficiently so to have blended in to the background of American suburban life, and not to have attracted any attention to themselves by the police, for example. This raises the old question as to whether there is an objective basis for referring to beliefs as being normal. Is there something cross-cultural about ideas of normality, or does normality only exist separately and differently in each culture, and each religion?

In this regard, understanding symmetrization suggests that normality is an ability to register similarity in the context of difference, and difference in the context of similarity. Thus, we have the man in Chapter 2 who couldn't register all the numerous differences between his brain waves and the waves that enter a wireless receiver, such as that carried by police, but could only register one or two similarities between them. On the other hand, we have the depressive in Chapter 4 who can't register the similarities between themselves and other people that are good and life affirming; they can only register differences and ones that are wholly disadvantageous to the depressed person. In a marriage, say, each partner is typically aware that they satisfy different needs and wishes that the other person has, whilst recognizing the context that there is the similarity that each satisfies some needs of the other person. In such a context, the differences and similarities between the two partners are seen and understood by each person. Neither sees only similarity and no differences or only differences and no similarities. The closest this comes to breaking down is typically in a marital quarrel, when one typically feels that she or he is doing pretty well all the giving, and the other pretty well all the taking. Usually, once the quarrel has subsided each partner recognizes the unreality of some, at least, of what they said during the quarrel. It is this later perception of unreality of what was said during the quarrel which allows the marriage to survive.

I argued earlier that symmetrization is an outcome of abstraction, but I said nothing about what idea of abstraction I was using. I will now attempt to repair this gap by noting the remark of the philosopher Hegel, who once asked, "Who thinks Abstractly?" and he answered his own question by saying, "The market woman. She sees in the customer someone to be cheated." In other words, the market woman only sees the customer very one-sidedly, and that is what it is to be abstract. In that case, *to be concrete must be the opposite of this, it must therefore be all-roundedness.* To be concrete in this sense of the word is to see similarities in the context of differences and differences in the context of similarities.

This is a different kind of "concrete" from saying that a table is "concrete," which is the usage of concrete that we usually have in English, but there is in the dictionary a sense of concrete which is of being "concatenated" or "all put together." Indeed, with these ideas of abstract and concrete we can form an idea that you can't form otherwise, something that sounds very odd at first, namely that of a *concrete abstraction.*

An example of a concrete abstraction is the growth of our understanding of history. Originally, history was just a record of monarchs and battles, then economic history was added, then social history, then cultural history; more recently, labor history, gender history, history of science, linguistics and discourse history. As a result, the study of history has become more concrete in the sense of all-rounded with all these types of history having an immensely complex interrelation with each other. At the same time, all these aspects of history are abstracted from the fact that a human individual only exists because a functioning human body supports a functioning human brain which also supports a functioning human consciousness. The contents of these types of history operate in abstraction from those biological details. Though I myself am a non-racist, I think it is instructive to see what a racialist's criticism of this would amount to. S/he would say that some relevant details of human biology were being thus missed, and the claim would then be that such accounts of history were inadequately concrete. That is, the racist would be claiming that those accounts of history which omitted certain details of human biology, which the racialist took to be important, had abstracted from them, and was to that extent an abstract abstraction. However, as details of human biology seem in fact not to change, racialists have always been unable to explain change in history, such as the growth in the proportions of girls getting school-leaving qualifications in mathematics approximately doubling in the last thirty years of the twentieth century, without apparently any change in their biology.

This discussion of concreteness is about seeing differences in the context of similarities and similarities in the context of differences. By contrast, to only at some moment see similarity, or only difference, is an *abstract abstraction.* Someone who believes in the existence of something which is only different from all else, like God, for example, is engaging in abstract abstraction; the abstraction here is that all the attributes of God are good attributes, so an abstraction has occurred from all the bad attributes that exist. God is, therefore, a very one-sided entity, and is, therefore, an abstract abstraction. The very odd-looking beliefs of people with schizophrenia are abstract abstractions as are the beliefs of those with depression.

Abstract abstraction can also occur outside psychosis, in extreme situations in daily life, such as the shocked sense of loss of people who lost a loved one in the World Trade Center due to the attacks of September 11th. The feeling is at first very one-sided—just grief, pure grief, and it feels unbounded, or infinite. But for most people, the loss will gradually be confronted, the period of grief will end, and those left behind will get on with their lives as best they can. Their post-grief situation will become like that of any other normal person who experiences all manner of feelings, emotions and the like, and each of us makes our own linkages to all manner of feelings. To pass through a period of mourning and return to normal consciousness is to *make an ascent from the abstract to the concrete.* It is very painful, for it involves letting go of the lost one(s). But ultimately, life can't go on if one-sided attention to that loss is not eventually balanced by other feelings, more life-affirming feelings than simply those of the loss. I will develop this further in a later chapter.

I am going to argue in the next three chapters that it is abstract abstraction which is what most frequently occurs in undemocratic or inadequately democratic political contexts. Two of these will be studies of the operation of symmetrization in two militantly anti-democratic instances of political thinking, namely that of the Nazis and of Karl Marx. I will then turn to the fascinating material from the Middle East, which is extremely rich in showing up the effects of abstract abstraction in the form of ignorant or evasive symmetrization, and the production of fantasied injustice.

Democracy, therefore, is that type of policy in which an ascent from the abstract to the concrete is most likely, and the challenges to racialist beliefs, sexist beliefs, homophobic beliefs, the recognition of the universality of child abuse, have all been examples of such an ascent. Our understanding of our social reality has become more concrete. Thus, it seems to me to be no accident that these ascents have occurred mostly in the liberal democracies. This, to my mind, only shows a fundamental superiority of this type of politics over all other kinds. If so, then whilst all cultures may in some abstract sense be of equal value, not all political cultures are of equal value.

II
Symmetries versus Liberal Democracy

7

Symmetries versus Liberal Democracy: The Case of Nazism

The day of the attacks on New York and Washington was some fifty-seven years after the liberation of the last of the Nazi death camps, but these places and the people who worked in them between 1941 and 1945 are not adequately understood, and our view of humanity as a result has not yet entirely got beyond all the errors of the Nazis. I am going to argue that part of the requisite understanding of Nazism that has been lacking up until now is how utterly Nazism was constructed from ignorant and evasive symmetrization. If this understanding helps explain Nazism, something many have found impossible up until now, then it will hopefully dispel any lingering belief that Nazism contains within it some hidden truth about human nature which most people are just too cowardly to confront. On the contrary, the net effect of this study will be to agree with Hannah Arendt's description of Nazism as the "banality of evil" and to locate it as an inauthentic infinity, as something humanity needs to transcend.

In Chapter 4, I worked up the idea of the difference infinity, and in Chapter 5, I applied this idea to the popular religious perception of heaven and hell. Recall that the picture of heaven was of a place infinitely above us in some sense and everything in heaven was pictured as unboundedly or infinitely good. By contrast, our picture of hell is somewhere infinitely far below us and things in hell are pictured as unboundedly or infinitely bad. So both of these are infinities, where heaven is at positive or plus infinity, and hell is at negative or minus infinity. Between them, they constitute a pair of difference infinities.

With this in mind, I'll look at a couple of quotes from an early Nazi thinker, Houstan Stewart Chamberlain, (1855–1927). In a book entitled *The Foundations of the Nineteenth Century,* published in 1899, he wrote:

The world owes to the Romans its rescue from Semitic Asiatic spell, permitting predominantly Indo-Teutonic Europe to become the beating heart and thinking brain of all mankind.

And the Roman Empire itself collapsed in that:

The work of an incomparably energetic Indo-European race was revised and manipulated by the subtlest minds of the West Asiatic mixed races, this again leading to the obliteration of unity and character.

Or that the work of Teutonism:

is beyond all question the greatest that has hitherto been achieved by men.

The Jewish origins of Jesus Christ were flatly denied. "There was not a drop of Jewish blood in his veins!" exclaimed Chamberlain. Chamberlain attributed Ernest Renan's statement, *"Jesus etat un juif"* ("Jesus was a Jew") to Jewish tyranny and influence. (All quoted Louis L. Snyder (*The Encyclopaedia of the Third Reich,*) page 51.)

One could find plenty of other instances, but the pattern in Chamberlain is clear: there is total loss of any perception of similarity between Romans and Semites, or on the other hand, Indo-Europeans and Semites. Crucially, Chamberlain gave all the *positive attributes to the non-Jews and all negative attributes to the Semites, and in so doing he equated each people to one of their parts.* In other words, each image of Semite and non-Semite is via a whole-part symmetrization and each would thereby produce an infinity, except with the enormous difference that whereas the non-Semites would appear to be at plus infinity, to be heavenly so to speak, the Semites would appear to be at minus infinity. The non-Semites, or Aryans, thereby occupy a position of sublime value, whilst Jewishness becomes an infinity of degradation and filth.

So we see the operation of a kind of abstraction—namely an abstraction from disconfirming details, as the quotes show. The most sensational is perhaps the denial that Jesus of Nazereth was born Jewish—an excellent example of abstraction from disconfirming detail.

The *Protocols of the Learned Elders of Zion* is probably the most famous document within what I would broadly call the Nazi canon, and it too shows remarkable abstraction.

Thus, part of *Protocol 1* reads:

. . . people with corrupt instincts are more numerous than those of noble instinct. Therefore in governing the world the best results are obtained by means of violence and intimidation, and not by academic discussions. . . .

But then, in *Protocol 12,* we read:

Literature and journalism are two of the most important educational powers; for this reason our government will buy up the greater number of periodicals . . .

Well, which is it—violence and intimidation, and not by academic discussions, or by means of literature and journalism? The ability to believe both these propositions at the same time means that each functions as an abstract abstraction, completely split off

41

from each other. What is being held by the author of the *Protocols* to motivate the Jews is a malignant infinity, such as the pursuit of a malignant infinity of power, or of wealth, or of exploitativeness, etc. What in turn maintains this entire show on the road is the completely abstract way in which the word Jew operates; it has no single meaning, but what its usage in these texts has is a very, very unusual infinity, namely an infinity of (malignant) flexibility! This it must be, because literally any (malignant) allegation can be made against Jews or Jewishness, and this is only possible if these are given an infinite flexibility by these authors. Here is perhaps the most remarkable way in which Jews and Jewishness are held to be different from all others; in short via a difference infinity. It is via such an infinity of difference that Jews can be portrayed as being different from all others by being infinitely sinister. We see how the Nazi world outlook is via symmetrization, *sui generis*. The Nazi outlook just could not exist at all without symmetrization; that and the existence of symmetrization via abstract abstraction is the secret of the Nazi theory of Jews and Jewishness. Of course, if symmetrization was the secret of Nazi theory, the gas chamber was the secret of ultimate Nazi practice, as it gradually evolved.

Within the Nazi belief system itself, we readily see how the claims against the Jews involved one abstract abstraction after another. Take the claims that (a) Germany lost the First World War because it was "stabbed in the back" by the Jews, and (b) the Russian Revolution of October 1917 was part of a World Jewish Conspiracy. Firstly, so far as the German army in its final battles in 1918 had as much equipment as before, and was under the command of von Hindenburg and von Ludendorff as before, it fought as well as it ever had. Secondly, the very victory of the Bolsheviks in Russia in 1917 actually increased the chances of Germany winning the war, because Germany was suddenly free to fight on its Western Front only! So, if the Bolshevik Revolution was inspired by the World Jewish Conspiracy, it was one that very nearly enabled Germany to win the First World War! That's how racially anti-German these supposedly conspiratorial Jews were being in 1918!

The other main belief in the Nazi German state was of course the Aryan man, and to see a little of what this involved I'll quote the following brief examples:

Since the so-called Aryans were thought to be at a heavenly plus infinity, only architecture which exemplified this status would be appropriate. Louis L. Snyder (*The Encyclopaedia of the Third Reich,* page 10) records how Hitler liked really massive buildings, like the Vienna Opera House, and as for Berlin:

Berlin must change its face to adapt to the new mission.

In this connection the new Berlin was to have:

. . . two huge north-south and east-west axes. Colossal railroad stations were to be built in the North and the South. The main plaza was crowned by an Arch of Triumph, planned to rival Napoleon's *Arc de Triomphe* in Paris. Sighting through its 260 foot opening, the visitor would see the end of the three mile vista the Great Hall with its enormous dome . . . a town hall 1500 feet long . . . a cinema seating two thousand people . . .

This was an architecture reeking of infinity to reflect an infinitely sublime people. What else could such an infinitely valuable race be but the true master race? For, if one interpreted the ideas of evolution to be a murderous *survival of the fittest* between different races, what else was appropriate except that the master race show its infinite superiority by killing or enslaving all racial inferiors? However, for the master race to win actual mastery would also need an infinity of hardness. So we understand why, as Snyder, page 11, records that Hitler decreed that:

43

True German art must never depict anguish, distress or pain.

Such feelings were asymmetries to the symmetrization that constructed the master race, and must accordingly be symmetrized out.

As for the negative infinity of Jewishness, that's what the Holocaust was supposed to affirm, and even celebrate.

Of course other symmetrizations were at work in the Nazi system. All legitimacy came from whatever the state with infinite flexibility decreed it to be, and any individuality which in any way dissented from this was brutally symmetrized out. There are many examples of this in the Nazi era but I'll quote just one. In *A Social History of the Third Reich,* Pelican Books, 1971, Richard Grunberger quotes an instance during the war about a German who kept a diary in which he recorded that he thought in about 1943 or thereabouts that Germany was going to lose the war. He recorded this thought in his diary, but in the course of an air raid, he was separated from his diary, which someone else found, and handed in to the Gestapo. The Gestapo went through his diary, found his remark, and then traced the diary to its owner. When questioned, the diary owner readily agreed that he had written the remark, but said he had done nothing wrong as he hadn't said what he had written to anyone, so he hadn't undermined the morale of the war effort in any way. But the Gestapo still got him—on a charge of "self-sabotage," sabotaging his own morale! How is that for an example of symmetrization, where the state has infinite flexibility in deciding what is legitimate? Note also those vast columns of marching German soldiers in which the Nazis so gloried; were they not supposed to exude just such a symmetrization, which then produced its fantasized infinities of order, rationality and invincibility?

To the Nazi system, any valid disagreement with something said by the Leader was symmetrized out. One result of this loss of asymmetries was that any statement by the Leader could seem infinitely justified, infinitely reasonable. Such a person was thus no ordinary, fallible chap, but the agent of an (infinite) Fate, as he liked to invoke.

So, perhaps for the first time, we begin to acquire an actual explanation of something endlessly said to be inexplicable, namely the vast Nazi massacres and the ability of people to carry them out, to guard the concentration camps, to operate the gas chambers themselves and so on. People whose image of Jews was of an infinity of degradation and filth could carry out such acts, and could think of the gas chambers as fumigation against lice and other pests. To maintain this symmetrization of course required vigorous censorship, which symmetrized out any mention of any similarities between Aryan and Jew. Indeed it seems as if many millions of Germans were terrorized into not even thinking of any similarities. Rigorous censorship maintained these fantasized difference infinities.

There is a further point. Recall the argument that it is infinity that is seductive. Enough Germans found Nazism very seductive, and were seduced into supporting it. A doctrine that put the Germans at plus infinity did the trick.

So far as the period between 1933 and 1945 is concerned, we need merely note that although the Jews were not the only people to suffer from Nazi murdering on a huge scale, the Jews were the people who were marked out by the Nazis with the greatest difference from so-called Aryan people. Via the theory I've just developed, that *totality of difference between Jew and non-Jew* is central to the whole Nazi world outlook. By contrast, killing Russians, homosexuals, Romanies or Rosicrucians was much less central to the Nazi project: images of them were not wholly via pairs of difference infinities.

Meanwhile, what of the post-1945 situation? The Jewish religion contains six hundred and thirteen commandments, and the Jewish thinker, Professor Emil Fackenheim, has argued that since

1945, Judaism has needed a six hundred and fourteenth commandment, namely: "Do not give Hitler any posthumous victories." But without the concept of symmetrization, and the way in which a pair of symmetrizations can produce a pair of difference infinities, I would argue that that is exactly what has been happening, and it's been happening for over half a century now. For every time someone, usually Jewish, has said that the Holocaust is inexplicable, that is exactly what they did—gave a posthumous victory, because a Nazi would find this claim of inexplicability of the Holocaust very encouraging and would say something like:

> With your superficial Jewish rationalism, of course you can't understand the depths of the Aryan soul, its infinite difference, its ineffable unknowingness to some Jewish subhuman.

There has been the added difficulty of those (mostly Jewish thinkers) who have tended to be most concerned at thinking about the Holocaust, that the ability to think about the Holocaust has been attacked by the veritable crescendo of pain, suffering, savagery and loss, which has just gone on and on and on and which has left all these feelings utterly unbounded, completely without limit. Without the explanation of symmetrization, this discourse has itself just gone on and on and on, seemingly unable to obtain closure. But through the concept of symmetrization, I think that we can finally surmount the banal, inauthentic infinities of Nazism, and give conceptual closure at any rate.

One pair of difference infinities, those allegedly defining Jew and Christian, has long had a famous attack on it in English, namely by Shylock in *The Merchant of Venice,* Act III, Scene 1:

> . . . Hath not a Jew eyes? Hath not a Jew hands, organs, dimensions, senses, affections, passions? Fed with the same food, hurt with the same weapons, subject to the same diseases, healed by the

same means, warmed and cooled by the same winter and summer as a Christian is? If you prick us do we not bleed? If you tickle us do we not laugh? If you poison us do we not die?

Such similarities between Jew and Christian are of course asymmetries to the pair of symmetrizations that construct a pair of difference infinities. That is why the similarities quoted by Shakespeare de-infinitize these infinities, and Shylock wins his point.

I conclude that its only by means of the concept of symmetrization that we can actually get to grips with Nazi theory, and we need to do this; firstly, to know how to fight the preconditions that would allow any new Nazi movement to get going. But, secondly, we need to get on top of the Holocaust if humanity is ever to get beyond the Nazis, if the Nazis are to be deprived of a posthumous victory, of having destroyed secular humanity's best hopes. So far, since 1945, I think we haven't done that, but I think that by means of symmetrization we can begin to fight back. Incidentally, if the concept of symmetrization and what it gives rise to can do this, then this approach is not just another way of saying something explicable in other words, it is actually a new concept with explanatory powers that other concepts lack.

I conclude that via all the concepts developed here we can acquire increased understanding of how it was that the world's most formally educated people, the Germans, produced enough people who believed enough of the Nazi fantasies before 1933, so as to make the Nazis the biggest political party in the Germany prior to 1933. If one goes further and asks why symmetrization and its infinities did not operate in the same way in, say, Britain and France, then my answer is that Germany had never had the kind of straight victory of capitalism that occurred in England via the English Civil War, 1640–1660, or in France via the French Revolution. Capitalist norms which respect the individual have to dominate culturally for liberal democracy to dominate politically.

This previous thought only adds to my conclusion that the attractiveness of Nazi banality to millions of Germans and others has revealed no terrible, timeless, but hitherto concealed secret of the human condition, that there is no inherent reason arising from the huge Nazi inhumanities for a predominant pessimism about our species and its possibilities.

8

Symmetries versus Liberal Democracies: The Thinking of Karl Marx

It is interesting to observe that the group who carried out the attacks of September 11th was not wholly unlike a communist party of old. Both communists and those who carried out the attacks of September 11th were allegedly fighting on behalf of the *Wretched of the Earth.* Those who had carried out the attacks were university graduates, just like Marx, Lenin, and Fidel Castro had been in their day. Like the old communists, the attackers too look forward to a world of universal brotherhood and peace, to be achieved this time by conversion of all of humanity to Islam, and although it had never occurred to the old communists to actually call America the Great Satan, they did think that life under American capitalism was something of a hell, and that the actions of American governments were usually held to be pretty satanic.

If, for communists, American capitalism was the Great Satan, the Soviet state was something like a secular equivalent of God; recall that the God of the three monotheisms has attributes of omnipotence, omniscience and infinite justice. The Soviet state had total control of society, so was practically *omnipotent.* To be able to rationally control the whole economy in the interests of all, it would also need to be able to acquire all necessary economic information to do this, and so it would have to make out that it was *omniscient* in this matter. Finally, defenders of the Soviet state would make out that it was the nearest thing on earth to *infinite jus-*

tice. So it is not surprising that those who used to support Soviet power seemed boundlessly confident of its beneficence, that it possessed only good attributes, that it showed no signs of any fundamental problems itself, and any apparent problems were but the growing pains attendant on the over-fulfillment of the five-year plan by a joyful and enthusiastic work force, who thereby showed a striking daily contrast with the life of alienation and exploitation attendant on the continuation of world capitalism with its lackeys and imperialist running dogs. Certainly this confidence had seemed in its day to be entirely unbounded and hence infinite.

These were the make-believe infinities of Soviet practice, but were there any serious symmetrizations in how Dr. Marx himself thought about capitalism? Let's see. The basic organization in capitalism is the firm or corporation and Marx tacitly took it that a corporation does whatever it chooses to do out of self-interest. If this was so, then the fact that a corporation chose to employ someone must mean that the corporation took it to be in its self-interest to do so. In that case, to employ that person must be profitable for that corporation. But then, what the corporation paid that employee would have to be less in value than that person's contribution to the income of the corporation. In other words, the efforts or labor of that person, must, in association with other employees, create more value for the corporation than the corporation pays all the employees. Dr. Marx implicitly claimed that slogans like, "A fair day's pay for a fair day's work" tacitly equated that greater value that resulted from that employment to the lesser value of the wages or salaries paid. A whole was being equated to one of its parts, and so slogans like, "A fair day's pay for a fair day's work" were whole-part symmetrizations. What infinities of hate, loathing and contempt this discovery induced in Marx! And not only in him, but his millions of followers, too, for here in this difference between the two instances of value was the alleged origin of profit. Since corporations continually sought after profit, how to expand their profits, how to maximize their profits, how to protect their profits, what they struggled day and night to protect and expand was, tacitly, exploitation! Since the corporations undoubtedly continue to have legal ownership of all the profit that they have, and these laws of property do indeed apply to everyone in society, *all of society* then came to be seen by the communists as saturated with exploitation.

Marx tacitly proceeded to use his conclusion that the employers obtained more value than they paid for, as a crucial symmetrization. This I think he did because he then equated *all* the benefit that some employee derived from living in a liberal capitalist country with the value of that worker's wage or salary. But the benefit of living in liberal capitalism tends to be so much more than just wage packets, and could be seen to be so even in Marx's day. For example, commodity production in agriculture had for the first time abolished famine for those whose food was produced in a commodity way. Yet it had been common to have a famine about once a decade in Europe before about 1600 when the gains of commodity production began to stop this.

In our own day, of course, capitalism has brought the relative security in which most people in the urbanized (capitalist) countries live, its relative longevity, its relative freedom from pain, reduced the appalling pains and early deaths frequently endured by women over the centuries due to unwanted pregnancies, and allowed the free-speech traditions of liberal capitalism which has introduced an unprecedented rigor of argument which in turn re-enforces the above gains. Then, there has been capitalism's eventual abolition of slavery, the application of rigor to relations between the sexes which has done more than has ever been done before to reduce sexism, wife-beating and child abuse. All these examples show how Marx's tendency to treat capitalism as a story of one or another kind of exploitation is a gross symmetrization: it treats all relationships under capitalism as exploitative simply because of the exploitative nature of some of those relationships, in particular the wage relationship in which the total value of wages

51

and salaries paid by a corporation to all its employees is indeed less than the total value created within that corporation by all those employees. So, here was one crucial whole-part symmetrization in the thinking of Marx, and it generated what he took to be his justified infinity of hate and rage towards capitalism.

There was another striking symmetrization of the socialist movement and that related to the socialist red flag. This symmetrization occurred amongst opponents of socialism who often equated the redness of the Socialist flag with the redness of blood running in the streets. Redness of flag equaled redness of blood. That's how all socialism was equated with bloody revolution; by means of a symmetrization. However, the choice of red doesn't make the left very clever in relating to the feelings of the people it was trying to recruit. There are a good dozen colors from which to choose, but the left chose the color of blood. This derived from the left in the French Revolution which chose red because it was at the opposite end of the light spectrum from the Royal Blue of the French monarchy. But if unconscious processes work by means of abstraction, the political effect of this left-wing choice was disastrous, and gave an enormous help to conservatism. The process which equated the red flag with red blood was one which occurred unconsciously, although the outcome was conscious. That is exactly why it seemed so normal to so many people, why no argument could refute it. Conscious argument distinguishing red blood from well-meaning socialist red didn't and doesn't prevent unconscious functioning symmetrizing the two.

Meanwhile, so widespread was the wholesale rejection of capitalism that, like many people of my generation, I can remember a time when one third of humanity lived under a Soviet-style system. If, as I have argued, Marx's criticism of capitalist society as a whole was based on a whole-part symmetrization, then the communist movement was the biggest political seduction of my generation. The infinity of righteousness of the communist movement was an inauthentic infinity.

On September 11th, political Islam was the nearest thing that humanity had to a world socialist movement. When the Muslims got a political party going in Turkey they called it the Welfare Party, and to give to the poor—*zakkat* as it is called—is one of the five basic religious duties incumbent on each and every affluent Muslim. This is all good socialist stuff.

One infinity that easily derives from symmetrization is an infinity of innocence, and the peaceable daily observance of a religion easily produces this infinity of innocence in respect to that religion. Thus, the Nazis practiced wars of extermination and enslavement by the master race, the Marxists attempted to invoke the agency of a revolutionary working class, Islamic militants believe that "Islam is the solution to the problems of modern man," and so attempt to convert everyone to Islam, whilst America thinks that the task of spreading the benificence of liberal capitalism is best entrusted to the World Trade Organization. The methods of the first two of these four stood discredited on the day of the attacks in New York and Washington, but this was a lot less true on that day of the latter two. I shall now turn and look at what on September 11th was a notorious impasse between Jews and Muslims, namely the situation in the Middle East.

9

Symmetries versus Liberal Democracy: The Case of the Middle East

I have argued that the thinking of the Nazis and that of Marx operated politically via one or more serious symmetrizations, and that liberal democracy is the only form of state power in which the seductive infinities which result from such symmetrization are most likely to be resisted. The case of the relationship between Israel and her Arab neighbors offers much rich material with which to consider this question further, so rich indeed that I can only offer a few glimpses of it. Israel has been a liberal democracy since its foundation in 1948, but can such a democratic state be any more successful in containing the convictions that other people are out to destroy you when it has indeed had fifty years of more or less continuous attack? What about Israeli democracy versus the growth of Jewish theologically-justified thuggery which wishes to drive out those Arabs in the West Bank who obstruct the fantasy that this land was divinely given for dominant Jewish occupation?

It is common to refer to "the Middle East conflict," but I say that this phrase is itself a serious symmetrization. Whilst there certainly *has* been conflict, and there still *is* conflict, this is only a part of the story, and to speak of the whole situation as "the Middle East conflict" is therefore to equate the whole situation with just one of its parts. Thus, I will argue that the conflict is maintained by a good deal of collusion, but this, in turn, is something that the two sides further collude in denying. This chapter will demonstrate this; it will demonstrate the operation of a new kind of symmetrization, namely that which occurs when two sides agree to evade the same thing. This will show the operation of *collusive symmetrization*. It operates because each side pretends that its behavior is completely different, only different, as compared to the behavior of the other. The collusive symmetrization will be the joint denial of culpable similarities. To show this, I must show that each side is doing this, and for this purpose I will label each half of my arguments with an a.-Jews or a b.-Palestinians.

A Least Unjust Settlement

Before proceeding, I must explain what I think is the least unjust outcome of this situation between the Israeli and Palestinian peoples. My suggestions are based on a liberal, democratic, secular approach to the situation. Only in this way can *politics* operate between the two peoples, i.e. be a *political accommodation* between the two peoples.

Firstly, there is no such thing as an accommodation which will be wholly just to both sides; that hope or aim is just a symmetrization. All we can work for is a minimally unjust solution. Evidently, both Israelis and Palestinians deserve to live safe lives in as viable a state as possible, and each deserves to have its homeland feelings respected as far as possible. But both will have to make considerable changes.

Firstly, the Palestinians will have to accept that realistically most of the 3.6 million refugees whom they claim exist from the 1948 war and their descendants won't be returning to Israel. This is a very big thing for the Palestinians to accept. Imagine when the United Nations set up Israel in 1947 that they had said that only one quarter of the world's Jews could go and live there. We'd still be hearing about it today. Yet, by accepting that most of their refugees won't be returning to Israel, the Palestinians will be compelled to accept that perhaps only a quarter of the world's Palestinians will live in Israel itself. It's a very big change for them to make.

Israel, too, is going to have to make changes that will cause loud squeals of Israeli protest. Firstly, home is not a place where the armed forces of another state drive along the roads shooting at whom they wish. So, if the West Bank and the Gaza Strip are to be home to the Palestinians, then Israel can't continue to own the roads through those places so that its armored vehicles will still be able to drive along those roads at will. Accordingly, any Israeli settlers who continue to live in the West Bank and the Gaza Strip will have to do so with the permission of the future government of Palestine. So, Israel will broadly have to withdraw more or less to the boundaries of 1967 except that it will have to own and control a couple of roads so as to guarantee Jewish access to the Jewish site at the Western Wall.

The present situation where the Israelis have allocated around 80 percent of the water supply and 80 percent of Jerusalem to themselves, is something that will clearly have to come a lot closer to fifty-fifty share out. For either side to have 80 percent of the water in semi-desert conditions is not a peace-term. In short, a political accommodation can only be that if it leads to something like a normal relation of give and take between Israelis and Palestinians. What follows is going to be my examination of the obstacles which have so far prevented such a political accommodation; each will turn out to be a symmetrization.

I will examine these obstacle symmetrizations within two main periods in time: 1948–1988 and from 1988 onwards. The reason why 1988 is so important is because it was in December 1988 that the Palestinians took the crucial step of, formally at least, recognizing the right of Israel to exist. True, it took them another eight years to finally remove from their charter the clause requiring Israel's destruction, but in the meantime Israel had reciprocated the Palestinian move by formally recognizing the right of the Palestinian nation to have a state, too. This Israel tacitly did at Oslo in 1993.

Symmetrization Number One: Denial of Legitimate Existence, 1948–1988

During this period, each side denied that the other had a legitimate existence. Neither was justified in this claim, but each engaged in it, and there was therefore collusion in agreeing that either side had the right to deny legitimate existence to the other. Let us look at the details of this collusion.

1a. Israel's Denial of Palestinian Legitimacy

It was Israel Zangwell who first formulated what became the frequently invoked Zionist slogan—the Jews were a "people without land" and Palestine was a "land without people." This last was false, of course, at the time that Zangwell first formulated the maxim. Arabs had lived there for centuries and were doing so as the early Zionist congresses met from 1897 onwards. So, there was one denial of existence, or of right to existence, in Palestine.

Another denial of Palestinian legitimacy occurred via the Israeli claim that there had been radio broadcasts in 1948 urging Arabs to leave. Strikingly, no details of these alleged broadcasts have ever been produced; thus on what frequencies were these alleged broadcasts transmitted, who were the announcers, which radio station or stations allegedly broadcast the alleged messages, how many Arabs in the Palestine of 1948 even had radios, and why did a study of the archives of the Voice of America and the BBC World Service in 1961 fail to discover any of these alleged broadcasts, a fact published as long ago as May 1961 in the *Spectator* magazine in London? By means of the claim of these broadcasts, the Israelis made the case that most Arabs had left the territory of what became the state of Israel voluntarily, and thereby gave up all rights of residence on, or ownership of, that land. Israel also tended (before Oslo in 1993) to flatly deny that there was such a thing as a Palestinian nation; thus, Israeli Prime Minister Golda Meir claimed not to know of the existence of "the Palestinians."

1b. Muslim Arabs Deny Legitimacy of Israel on Muslim Arab Land

The establishment of Israel occurred on land on which Muslim Arabs had lived for centuries, on which hundreds of mosques had been built and so on. Did Muslim Arabs indeed owe Jews a piece of their own Muslim Arab land, on which Jews could have their own little homeland? They thought not.

However, I say that there are two reasons why Arabs did owe Jews a piece of land on which to have their own state. The first is that the main religion of the Arabs is Islam, and Islam does not believe in one person one vote equality between Muslims and non-Muslims. Islam is centered on the Islamic community, the Umma, and a Jewish community may exist within the Islamic one provided it accepts the political dominance of the Umma. Islam has a name for such a status, namely, the dhimmi status; this means being dominated politically by a government which by definition you had no hand in choosing, and is the kind of life that people of Indian origin had under apartheid in the old South Africa. Here is the first reason then why Muslim Arabs, by the end of World War II (when it was clear that the departure of the colonial powers of Britain and France was imminent) should not have denied the 800,000 Jews who lived in Arab countries of a piece of land for their own state. The fact that this is something long standing within Islam means it is not readily subject to change, which strengthens my point. Indeed inasmuch as Islam lacks any center comparable to the Vatican, what central body within Islam could ever modify this?

There is a second and parallel reason for my belief that Muslim Arabs owed the 800,000 Jews in their midst a piece of their own land. A polity in which the main moral system of that polity cannot be questioned is a polity which operates at a lower level of intellectual and moral honesty. Thus, in how many of the fifty-odd member countries of the Organization of the Islamic Conference can one publicly refute verses of the Qur'an, such as Sura 5, Verse 33 to 35 which has been rendered into English by Mr. N.J. Dawood as follows:

> Those that make war against God and His apostle and spread disorder in the land shall be slain or crucified or have their hands or feet cut off on alternate sides or be banished from the land. They shall be held up to shame in this world, and in the world to come grievous punishment awaits them: except those that repent before you reduce them. For you must know that God is forgiving and merciful.

Thus, on September 11th, a lecturer in a Pakistan medical school, Dr. Younis Shaikh was sitting on death row in a prison in Islamabad. The reason was that Dr. Shaikh had said, or was alleged to have said, in a lecture at his medical school, that Mohammed only became a Muslim when he received his first vision in about 610 of the Common Era. This is capable of being held to be blasphemy because Islam implies that it is the continuation of what was divine in Judaism and Christianity and so Islam can be claimed in some sense to have always existed. So, Dr. Shaikh was sentenced to death and was on death row as the U.S. worked to bring Pakistan into line with its campaign against terrorism following the attacks of September 11th.

It might be observed that the situation of Dr. Shaikh is in Pakistan which is not part of the Middle East, nor is it peopled by

59

Arabs. But where are the fatwas denouncing this death penalty, where are the resolutions of the Organization of the Islamic Conference attacking this outcome, which surely there would be if Muslim opinion were outraged by this action? Three months after the attacks of September 11th, the Organization of the Islamic Conference was reported on 10th December 2001 to have criticized Israel for its behavior towards the Palestinians; such criticism is evidently acceptable, but fatwas and resolutions from Islamic institutions condemning the passing of the death penalty for blasphemy are not. All this is in addition to the points I made in Chapter 6 about the inability to query in public whether a verse like Sura 23, verse 1 from the Qur'an does not license forms of barbarism.

I should add that I am *not* in agreement with the Prime Minister of Italy who, a couple of weeks after the attacks of September 11th, said that European culture was superior to that of Islam. That is making a statement about a *whole* culture, or group of cultures, namely all those which have Islam as their religion. I am only referring to one or two attributes of those cultures, so to think that I am making some statement about the *whole* of those cultures is false. To do so, in my opinion, would be a classic example of equating a whole, namely a whole culture, in this case, with one of its parts. Thus, one way in which Islamic culture is in fact superior to a Western culture is Islam's care of the poorest members of society. If we had two cultures of comparable economic wealth, one Islamic and one Western, I have little doubt that the Islamic would be the more caring of its poorest people.

Nevertheless, if societies in which Islam is the dominant religion wish to operate at the level of intellectual and moral honesty that I was referring to, then that is their current choice. But they do not have the right to force Jewish culture, whose own level of public honesty in matters of religion at least, and sometimes in other matters of public life, is respectable, to live within such a sub-honest polity. Here is a second reason that Muslim Arabs owed Jews a small piece of their Muslim Arab land. Israel is in any case a tiny one-thousandth part of the Middle East and has no important amounts of oil in it. So, there was no serious economic loss for the Arab and Islamic world in allowing Israel to exist.

The apparent non-existence of fatwas condemning the treatment of Dr. Shaikh certainly seems to be a striking silence. But it is hardly the first such case. A mufti within Sunni Islam is a specialist in religious law, the Sharia, whose opinion is sought on interpretations of that law. There was one such Mufti, the Mufti of Jerusalem, who collaborated with the Holocaust, and who actually had pleasant meetings with Hitler several times whilst the Holocaust was in progress, and he seems to have known broadly about the Holocaust. The Mufti was trusted enough by the Nazis to actually broadcast over Nazi radio from Berlin on the 21st September 1944, in the course of which he referred to "the eleven million Jews of the world," according to Bernard Lewis in his book *Semites and Anti-Semites,* 1997, page 157. The fact that the Mufti knew that there were just eleven million Jews left in 1944, compared to around sixteen or seventeen million in 1939, is striking. He may have been the only non-European to have known this in September, 1944 and presumably this information came from his agreeable fireside chats with his pal Adolf. There was striking lack of fatwas against his behavior from within Islam after 1945. Apparently having amiable chats with the originator and main driving force behind the Holocaust is, in practice, in no way contrary to the teachings of Allah the Compassionate.

There is further striking behavior towards Jews by Muslims. Between 1948 and 1967, no Jew from Israel was able to pray at the Western Wall as this wall lay in Arab East Jerusalem. Imagine if Israelis took this behavior by Muslims as a cue and said that no Muslim living in Israel could visit the Al Aqsa Mosque, or undertake the pilgrimage or Haj to Mecca! One may imagine what Israel would be accused of! By contrast, Jews unhesitatingly accept that the whole Mecca/Medina area must be entirely controlled by Mus-

61

lims for Muslims for as long as Islam exists. The matter in Jerusalem is more complex because Muslims built the Al Aqsa right on the site of the old Jewish Temple. This itself was an anti-Jewish action. Is this to be taken as yet a further example of how Islam has the solutions to the problems of modern man?

Symmetrization Number Two: The Right of Return

2a. Israeli Use of Right of Return

Officially, Israel was set up so that any Jew suffering persecution for his or her Jewishness could have a country to move to where this wouldn't happen; to give force to this, the very first law passed by the new Israeli parliament, guaranteed that any Jew could emigrate to Israel. But the law that guaranteed this was not something like a Jewish Freedom from Persecution Law or a Jewish Refugee law, or something of that ilk, but a Law of Return. In this way, two entirely different things were promptly conflated: freedom from persecution because of someone's Jewishness on the one hand, and a claim from the Jewish Bible that God gave this piece of land for dominant Jewish occupation on the other. The law had the advantage that no Jew wishing to move to Israel had to prove that they were being persecuted for being Jewish or was likely to be; but, by confounding the religious belief that the land is God-given to the Jews, with the fact of persecution, the Palestinians could deduce that having been displaced from the same land, they too should have a "right of return." The fantasy involved is best seen via the Palestinian usage of this.

2b. Palestinian Use of a Right of Return

If there is some secular "right of return" then naturally the Palestinians should invoke it, since they claim that there are some 3.6 million Palestinians who became refugees by being descended from those who were pushed out by Israel in 1948.

But is there such a thing as a "right of return"? Thus, do the Indian nations who used to have ancestral lands on what is now New York, Washington and Los Angeles have any practical right of return, to reclaim these areas? Does the Cherokee nation, so brutally pushed off their land in the American state of Georgia in the 1820s, when gold was discovered on their land, have any practical right of return? Then again, do the Parsees who now live in India and who were expelled from Iran centuries ago have a right of return to ancestral land in Iran? Do the Berber peoples, who inhabited the coast of North Africa from Egypt to the Atlantic for some 2000 years until the Arab conquest of North Africa in the seventh century CE, which drove the Berber peoples inland towards the Atlas Mountains, have a "right of return" to their ancestral coastal land? And what about the Matabele people who now live in Zimbabwe but whose ancestors, the Ndebele, used to live in what is now South Africa, before being driven out by the Zulu in the 1830s—do the Matabele have some "right of return" to ancestral lands in South Africa? My point is that from the fact that *some* peoples now live broadly on the land in which their peoplehood developed, such as the Russians or the Chinese or the British or the French or the Germans, does not mean that *all* peoples have some presumed right to do so. That would be a symmetrization of all the peoples with just some peoples. Obviously, that does contain some lack of equity between peoples, but it's a lesser one than would result from trying to move hundreds of millions of people around, to remake the map of human settlement.

Certainly, expulsion was the main way in which Jews came to control the land after 1948, but then had Muslim Arabs been prepared to allow Jews to have the sort of area of land awarded to the Israelis by the United Nations partition of 1947, for the reasons that I argued for above, Israelis wouldn't have had to engage in anything like as much expulsion. Whilst there plainly does deserve to be one state in the world which will protect any Jew from persecution, and Israel had to pass legislation to bring this about, to have framed that legislation as a Law of Return has enabled both Israelis and Palestinians to invoke an alleged "right of return" and to thereby wholly ignore the homeland needs and homeland feelings of the other people. The alleged "right of return" has thereby functioned as a symmetrization by each people of the homeland needs and homeland feelings of the other people and has massively obstructed the required political accommodation that each people owes the other.

Symmetrization Number Three: The Holocaust

3a. Israeli Use of the Holocaust

I gave two reasons in the preceding sections why Muslim Arabs owe Israel its existence, and in so doing I appealed to what I take to be undeniable facts of Arab and Islamic existence. By contrast, to brandish the Holocaust at the Arabs as the reason why they should allow Israel to exist on what had been land owned and worked by Muslim Arabs, amounts to treating Arab existence as if it was of no account. This is to treat the importance and indeed worth of such existence as a zero. This is, of course, a striking injustice to Arab existence. And, sure enough, as we have earlier noted in respect of injustice, it produces an infinity of Arab (and Islamic) indignation.

3b. Palestinian Use of the Holocaust

If Israeli use of the Holocaust has been a symmetrization, so, too, has been Palestinian use. It has enabled Palestinians and other Arabs to protest that in relation to Israel's existence on land which Muslim Arabs used to own and work, they the Arabs are just a victim, wholly victim, completely victim. That is, Muslim Arabs did not owe Jews any of their own land but they the Palestinians have been victimized by the European Holocaust of the Jews. In this way, the Palestinians use the Holocaust to evade admitting that there are reasons from within Muslim Arab society why they owed Jews a piece of their land.

If either side is criticized for their evasive use of the Holocaust, then each is prone to say, "Oh, you're blaming the victim." It is, therefore, well worth showing that this is a symmetrization.

Symmetrization Number Four: Pure Victimhood

Liberal society accepts that there are indeed *some* circumstances where there is an increase in injustice if the victim is blamed for the injuries suffered. Thus, there is the classic case of a rapist who tries to get acquitted at his subsequent trial by claiming that the woman he attacked was attractively dressed. But is *all* victimhood of this attacked-woman type? If I stepped into the road without looking, and was run down by a car, I would be the victim, but I should also be very much to blame for what happened to me. The difference here is surely the judgement that in stepping out into the road I made a *culpable* contribution to my injuries, whereas in liberal cultures, we judge that an attractively dressed woman makes no *culpable* contribution to the fact of sexual attack. So, the indignant accusation of "victim blaming" tries to pretend that *all* victims are of the attacked-woman type. As, in fact, only some are, we have symmetrization of all victims with just one type. The assumption in some circles that one must never blame the person who is most hurt from some situation is a taboo, and is also an excellent example of how taboos are often, and perhaps, always, evasive symmetrizations.

4a. The Victim Symmetrization by Jews

Jews do not have much difficulty pointing to events in Europe, especially during the twentieth century, which allow them to feel as if they were only victim, wholly victim, etc. But why that makes them just victims, only victims in relation to the Arabs of the Middle East, needs some further explanation. Of course, Arab opposition to Jewish emigration from Europe after 1933 did turn out to have monstrous consequences, something Arabs seldom acknowledge or for which they show the slightest regret. But that is still not a reason to say that the Palestinians don't deserve a state, painful as Jews find it to reflect on how many more might have been saved from the Holocaust but for Arab opposition to Jewish emigration to the then British colony of Palestine. Plenty of other peoples were just as disinterested in the plight of the Jews in the 1930s, and with less reason as they did not stand to lose land due to Jewish immigration as the Arabs of Palestine did.

4b. The Victim Symmetrization by Arabs

Some people would argue that Muslims have some justification in feeling victimized by the creation of the state of Israel on land on which Muslim Arabs used to own, when one considers that Jews under Islam did better than Jews in Christian Europe, certainly before the French Revolution of 1789 which led to Jewish Emancipation in Europe. But then, the Indians who lived under old-style apartheid in the old-style South Africa lived better than those who lived under the Muslim Idi Amin in Uganda, and in much of multi-racial Africa generally, and in fact the situation of a Jewish community under Islam is very similar to the position of a people like the Indians under old style apartheid in the old South Africa. Thus, historically, the Jewish communities that lived under Islam had to pay a special tax, because their sons didn't join the fighting forces of the Muslims, just like the Indians under apartheid weren't trained in the apartheid armed forces either. However, these examples are not much reason to think that an apartheid solution to Jewish existence in the Middle East would be an acceptable one.

The first nineteen years of Israel's existence contain another example of Arabs playing the victim-symmetrization. From 1948 to 1967, both the West Bank and the Gaza Strip were in Arab hands, the West Bank under Jordan, the Gaza Strip under Egypt. If the Arabs cared a fig for their Palestinian Arab brothers, why did they themselves not set up a Palestinian state, with a Parliament in Arab East Jerusalem, then under the control of Jordan? Of course, the refusal by most Arabs, it seems, at the time to recognize Israel's right to exist obviously contributed to this situation. For, had the Palestinians started their own state in the West Bank and Gaza Strip between 1948 and 1967, some people would have asked if this wasn't the beginning of a settlement with an Israel which might have some permanency, because Israel's own existence was thereby being tacitly admitted. Of course, compromise makes no sense to people who think that all the justification is on their side; that is what comes of symmetrizing *all* the justification with the *part* that your side equitably possesses. So, I conclude that the thing of which the Palestinians were most "the victim" is their own callous symmetrizations, namely those that symmetrized out from their minds what the Arabs owed the Jews. But, then, we have seen that the Israelis have been just as capable of callous symmetrizations of their own.

How These Symmetrizations Prevented
Politics from Operating

The symmetrizations that we have just discussed allowed each side to symmetrize out each other's justified existence and in the minds of each side created an infinity of justification for the position that each side took up. During these decades, the Arabs formally codified their opposition to the existence of Israel at a meeting in Khartoum on the 1st September, 1967 at which the Arabs declared a Policy of the Three No's: no recognition of Israel, no negotiation with Israel, no peace treaties with Israel.

Yet this may well have suited some Israelis down to the ground! Those who looked forward to a Greater Israel, e.g. in the West Bank, could have a freer hand, for if the Arabs wouldn't even recognize the Israeli right to exist, what had they to lose if they seized more Arab land? Arab objection? We thought you weren't talking to us! To refuse to talk to someone makes it difficult, in short, to state your objections to them personally. I claim that the Policy of the Three No's functioned as a collusive symmetrization. For those Israelis committed to expansion, the symmetrization allowed them to pretend that the expansion was not causing Israel additional problems with the Arabs, whilst the Arabs could continue to pretend that the entire existence of Israel was just a temporary affair. What was being collusively symmetrized out on both sides was any idea of a long-term normal relationship of give and take between Israeli and Palestinian.

These then were the leading symmetrizations during Israel's first forty years of existence, 1948–1988, and they tended to produce a lack of politics between Arabs and Israelis. The first state to formally break out of these mutual and collusive symmetrizations was Egypt.

Breaking the Mold

Until 1979, not a single Arab country recognized Israel's right to exist, but in that year, Egypt broke the mold and did so. This was formally followed by Jordan in 1995, but in the meantime, and very importantly, the Palestine Liberation organization, headed by Yasser Arafat, formally, at least, did the same thing. As the Palestinians had been the Arabs who had suffered most by the establishment of Israel, this decisive step in 1988 was a crucial breakthrough.

The Arab denial of Israel's right to exist was to some extent underwritten by the Soviet Union and its allies. It is, perhaps, no accident that the Palestinian recognition of Israel's right to exist should come at the end of the 1980s, as the Soviet political system was visibly starting to totter.

The Symmetrization of Ethnic Cleansing

There is another symmetrization which has become fashionable, namely the use by Palestinians and other Arabs of the term "ethnic cleansing" to describe Israeli behavior in the West Bank and Gaza Strip. Since the Bosnian Serbs started using the term ethnic cleansing in the mid-1990s to describe their policy of driving Bosnian Muslims off their land, Arabs have taken to saying Israel's foundation was an outbreak of ethnic cleansing, for instance in respect of some seven hundred thousand Arabs compelled or obliged to leave in 1948. However, the Bosnian Serbs of the 1990s were pushing Bosnian Muslims mainly off land so as to create a Greater Serbia, when Serbia already existed, its existence was respected. That was not Israel's situation in 1948, although Arabs were obliged to leave in 1948.

Israel and Apartheid: Another Symmetrization

It's also become fairly normal in Arab circles to talk of Israel as an apartheid state. By contrast, I would say that Israeli rule is only of a predominantly apartheid character in relation to the Palestinians in the West Bank and Gaza Strip. These frequently find themselves in the patrolling area of the Israeli police and Israeli army, but who have no vote in Israeli elections just as all blacks directly affected by apartheid lived within the patrolling area of the South African Police and South African Army, but had no vote for the old apartheid parliament either.

One important question here is, how long does such a situation go on? White South Africa compelled blacks to live decade after decade under a government from which they were barred from voting and which controlled the police force and army. The Palestinians of the West Bank and Gaza Strip have had over thirty-five years of this sort of situation. However, to say that all of Israel practices apartheid is, I will argue in my next chapter, a symmetrization: but on September 11th Israel was operating an apartheid protectorate in the West Bank and Gaza Strip. I deal with this more fully in the next chapter.

1988 to the Present

In December 1988, the Palestine Liberation Organization finally made a declaration officially accepting Israel's right to exist within internationally agreed borders. In practice, these seem to be broadly those of the 4th June 1967. Since Arabs had given up denying Israel's right to exist, it was up to Israel to reciprocate. This it tacitly did via the discussions in Oslo and the Agreement of 1993. Some Israelis and some Palestinians began to think seriously about a compromise; but not all, by any means. As one who supports such a compromise, I will now turn to looking at the positions of those on both sides who oppose such a settlement.

Palestinian Opposition to Oslo

The most coherent opponent of Oslo amongst the Palestinians is surely the militant Islamic organization, Hamas. This organization simply opposes the existence of Israel, and thinks that any Jewish community in the region should accept the traditional Islamic position of the dhimmi status.

Israeli Opposition to Oslo

Because Israel has strong democratic traditions, it doesn't have any directly comparable body to Hamas. Historically, the Jewish Irgun terrorist organization, run by Mr. Begin and Mr Shamir in the 1940s, was probably the nearest thing to Hamas that Jews have ever produced. However, four of Israel's prime ministers, Menachem Begin, Yitzchak Shamir, Binjamin Netanyahu, and Ariel Sharon might be loosely described as Herut prime ministers, men who broadly subscribed to the teachings of one of the pioneer Zionists, Zeev Jabotinsky. These teachings focus entirely on the needs of Jews in Israel, thereby denying the Palestinians any consideration of homeland needs and feelings, as Hamas has shown towards those of the Jews.

The Herut/Hamas Rejectionist Front

By contrast with Israel's Herut prime ministers mentioned above, the Israeli prime minister who had come nearest by September 11th of trying to satisfy the homeland needs of both sides

71

was Ehud Barak. Relative to the sort of agreement which Mr. Barak was gradually feeling his way towards, what we have in practice is a Herut/Hamas Rejectionist Front. This is an excellent example of a collusive symmetrization: what each of the two partners in this Front agree about is that they entirely reject the Barak-style political accommodation, Herut because it wishes to keep the overwhelming majority of settlements in the West Bank and Gaza Strip and expand them by perhaps 2 percent a year, and Hamas who simply wish to destroy Israel altogether. Accordingly, the very last thing either of these two organizations wish to see is their people's seal of approval to some international agreement which recognizes boundaries of the state of Israel and that of a viable Palestine alongside a viable Israel, in international law. The two organizations both symmetrize out this sort of accommodation: they are engaged in collusive symmetrization. The symmetrizations concerned produce the infinities of indignation and self-righteousness that are so noticeable on both sides; each of these two organizations specializes in believing that between them and the other side it's all a matter of difference, pure difference. Let us look at some instances of the collusion of the Herut/Hamas front:

The first major illustration of this front came during Israel's general election of 1996, the first Israeli election since the Oslo agreement came into force. During the election campaign, Hamas staged a mass killing of civilian Israelis, killing over fifty of them. Why? Because Labor Prime Minister Shimon Peres was being challenged by Herut leader Binjamin Netanyahu for the premiership of Israel. If my theory is correct, one would expect Hamas to greatly prefer Mr. Netanyahu, and sure enough, a bombing campaign in an election is bound to help a rightwing organization like Herut. The bombing campaign did indeed do just that and, given the small margin of Mr. Netanyahu's victory, it seems certain that Hamas's help made all the difference to his victory.

Mr. Netanyahu then proceeded to do what he promised,

72

which was broadly to try and stall on any further Oslo style "concessions" to the Palestinians, exactly as Hamas would wish. Israel's political stock fell heavily in the liberal countries, something which can only have given Hamas further pleasure.

This strategy of using killing of Israelis to topple an Israeli Labor Prime Minister and replace him with a Herut one was again seen when Labor Prime Minister Ehud Barak was being challenged by another Herut leader, this time Ariel Sharon, in 2001. Hamas's efforts to replace Mr. Barak with Mr. Sharon occurred in two phases. Firstly, in September 2000, Mr. Sharon visited the Al Aqsa Mosque complex in Jerusalem, and, inasmuch as Mr. Sharon was not known for his interest in, or acceptance of, the precepts of Allah the Compassionate, there would seem to be truth to the claim that his visit was deliberately provocative. What was the response of groups like Hamas? Why, they behaved as if they had been provoked! If people allege that someone's behavior is provocative, and those people then behave as if they had been provoked, then those people are colluding with the provocative person, for they thereby give that person the satisfaction that s/he sought. The collusion was again entirely successful: Mr. Sharon became Prime Minister of Israel some six months later. This outcome had been much helped by attacks on Israeli troops, who then fired back, killing Palestinians, including Palestinian children. The Palestinians reciprocated, and as already noted, the Herut/Hamas Rejectionist Front repeated in 2001 the success they achieved in 1996. My theory has further confirmation in that there was no such violence in the election of 1999, when Herut Prime Minister Binyamin Netanyahu was being challenged for the prime ministership by labor candidate Ehud Barak. Then, there was no campaign of shooting and killing Israelis by Hamas, who evidently didn't want Israelis to vote Mr. Netanyahu out. Nevertheless, they did, and both sides moved nearer to the sort of political accommodation sketched at the beginning of this chapter, especially at negotiations at the Egyptian resort of Taba in January

2001. It's safe to predict that when Mr. Sharon is next challenged by a Labor Israeli for Prime Minister, that again bodies like Hamas will not engage in any special level of shooting and killing of Israelis just as they didn't in 1999.

These collusive symmetrizations between Herut and Hamas of course continued after Mr. Sharon became Prime Minister in March, 2001. Palestinian militants continued with their killing, and Mr. Sharon then replied by saying he would not negotiate with *any* Palestinians until *all* Palestinians stopped the shooting and killing. That way, the Palestinian militant groups like Hamas and Islamic Jihad indirectly ran Israeli home and foreign policy. This outcome is an excellent illustration of the sort of outcome possible via collusive symmetrization.

Failure to Put Those Who Have Committed Terrorist Offenses on Trial

On the day of the September 11th attack, the air was thick with complaints by Israelis that the Palestinian leadership was failing to detain terrorists as Israel had repeatedly requested. However, never mentioned is the observation that in so behaving, the Palestinian leadership has followed the example set to them by founding Israeli Prime Minister, David Ben Gurion. For it was he who, after the State of Israel came into existence in May 1948, failed to arrest Mr. Begin and his followers, following the terrorist attack at Deir Yassin in which Jewish terrorists killed two hundred Arabs. This was at a time when Israel expected the new post-war Fourth French Republic set up in 1945 to arrest and try Frenchmen who had committed crimes against Jews between 1940 and 1944, i.e. before the Fourth Republic had existed. In short, as between Mr. Ben Gurion and Mr. Arafat, we have, in this matter of arresting one's own terrorists and putting them on trial for terrorism, another instance of collusive symmetrization: both condemn terrorism by their own people verbally, but neither has a history of rushing to arrest alleged terrorists from their side, nor to put such people on trial.

Mr. Arafat was guilty on September 11th of applying to Hamas and Islamic Jihad the same policies Mr. Ben Gurion applied to Mr. Begin and Mr. Shamir after 1948; but neither side will admit this, since each side pretends that between the two men it is a matter of pure difference, only difference, wholly difference. Both sides tacitly apply the difference infinity, and in this way both sides collude in symmetrizing out their culpable similarities.

Collusive Use of the Other Side's Killing

On September 11th 2001, Israelis complained loudly at killings of their civilians by Palestinians and Palestinians complained loudly at the killing of their civilians by Israelis. These complaints functioned as a further collusive symmetrization. Complaints about killing successfully destroy thinking about the necessary political changes in pretty well everyone whom I have met. That's why this analysis of what is needed for peace concludes that there must be a point blank refusal to predicate anything on the shooting and killing, or its ceasing. Any reference to it must be answered by asking what political changes are needed by each side, which can be seen to care for the homeland needs of both sides.

Portrayal of Shooting and Killing on Television

The problem that I have just discussed shows the way in which the shooting and killing are used by both sides to avoid making the political accommodation that a two-state solution will require. This evasive use of the shooting and killing is greatly aided by television, and indeed the whole idea of "the news." In this regard, let us recall the old cliché that "the camera never lies"; I say that this claim is in fact a vast symmetrization. To see this, consider television footage of, say, an Israeli tank firing shells at a school building containing Palestinian children; there seems to be no conceptual problem at first, if we take it that such footage arose from the very fact of the shelling. But what no television camera can photograph is the sub-political intransigence which produces shooting and killing. If the political intransigence on both sides is about equal, the fact that there are no Palestinian tanks to be photographed, but only Israeli ones, functions as a symmetrization. It thereby looks as if Israel is the cause of all the trouble. In fact, the problem doesn't end there: the symmetrization, by which this camera-symmetrization itself functions, can't itself be photographed: the power of abstraction must suffice.

Emotional Distance

Another unhelpful similarity between Israelis and Palestinians is the emotional distance between the two peoples. This emotional distance has, of course, been vital in the callous ignoring of the other people's homeland needs, which have existed on both sides. It will be one of the most unhelpful relationships once political accommodation commences, as it undoubtedly will. Each side will regard the changes it will have to make as enormous changes, whilst the changes made by the other side to accommodate them are regarded as trivial. Thus this symmetry only operates because enough people on both sides abstract from the homeland needs of the other people.

This lack of interest in the suffering of the needs of people on the other side could well have a very blatant outcome. This will come when—and it is only a question of when—a compromise agreement is eventually hammered out. So disinterested are so many people on both sides going to be in the needs of the people on the other side, that many will feel exceptionally bitter at the concessions that will inevitably have to be made. Indeed, it wouldn't surprise me if there aren't riots on both sides if and when a peace with long-term prospects of holding between the two sides finally does emerge. Israelis and Palestinians will be very lucky if discipline on both sides holds. An example of how it can hold was in the early 1990s when the African National Congress of South Africa and the outgoing white minority government of South Africa each held their political discipline over the great majority of their followers, as a settlement was hammered out.

Useful Things to Do to Help Bring about a (Concrete) Compromise

If this analysis is right, then it should be possible to list some practical steps that could ease the achievement of compromise. I suggest the following.

The shooting and killing could be used to fight back against the Herut/Hamas collaborators, as follows. On the first of June, 2001, an Islamic Hamas bomber left a large bomb in front of an Israeli night club and killed both himself and twenty Jewish teenagers. Contrast this with an event some ten years earlier when Rabbi Moshe Levinger, who was in charge of the Jewish settlement in the Palestinian town of Hebron, had shot dead a Palestinian shopkeeper, Kayed Hassan Salah, aged 42, standing in front of his shoe shop. The killer rabbi was not himself killed, so he could go on trial. He was put on trial by the Israelis, found guilty and got the entirely derisory sentence of about six months in prison from an Israeli court. (Source: Michael Sheridan in Jerusalem, *The Independent* (of London), 3rd May 1990. The same report quotes the Israeli judge in the case, Judge Shalom Brenner, as having said that the sentence "has to reflect the value of human life.") Where is the record in any book, with copies in both Hebrew and Arabic, of the dead shopkeeper? His name, his photograph, who his family is? How they've coped since his murder? Where is the same done for the families of the dead from the murder of 2001, too, and in similar details? That sort of publication, exposing the pain such killing causes, at regular intervals, in both main languages, might do something to get majorities on both sides to rein in their killers. This is something neither side has done much of, as I remarked earlier when discussing the religious organizations that both have been conspicuous in their absence in calling for the terrorists from their side to be put on trial and given heavy, life imprisonment sentences on conviction.

In both Judaism and Islam, each side mimics the other in being disinterested in the homeland needs and homeland feelings of the other side. Not all the most culpable people are religious; it's just that amongst the most culpable, those intensely committed to the maintenance of the Jewish religion and of Islam are extremely well represented. Thus, the militant Jewish settlers in the West Bank and Gaza Strip tend to be religious, and Hamas is the Islamic Resistance Movement. Perhaps the answer is that just as we need to detail the victims of terrorism on both sides in the same pamphlet, so, too, might we point out how the religious people on each side collude with religious people on the other side in using their God-given texts to function as a contemptuous dismissal of the needs and feelings of the other side.

Another way to fight the collusive symmetrization which I have been attacking, is for both Israel and the Palestinians to do some hard thinking about their democracy. Amongst the Palestinians, real democracy hardly seems to exist and as the material above so amply shows, I think, it badly needs to. This might have to await the passing of Yasser Arafat, although a conception of politics which speaks of Palestinian politics in terms of one man is, itself, amazingly undemocratic. Israel has colluded with that and added its own usage of the personage of Mr. Arafat to strengthen these pre-democratic tendencies in Palestinian society. As leader of the African National Congress of South Africa at the end of apartheid, Nelson Mandela was an exceptional man, but it was not due to him alone that the African National Congress government in post-apartheid South Africa has been a liberal democracy, with open criticism of the government in the press, and all shades of opinion tolerated, from communist to fascist.

Israel's democratic institutions, whilst superior to those of the Palestinians, are nevertheless not as infinitely superior to the Palestinian ones as Israelis like to think. Israel's democratic institutions have failed to be adequate to the tasks facing them, too. Firstly, Israeli democratic institutions have not been proof against manipulation by militant Islamists, as I observed when I discussed the outcomes of the Israeli elections of 1996 and 2001. Secondly, they failed to give Mr. Barak a decent four-to-five-year stint in which to try and come to an agreement with the Palestinians. Here is the main failure of the Israelis in 2001; the talks at Taba in January 2001 were broken off, and Mr. Barak was forced to stand for an election before he had had a chance to achieve a compromise. Not surprisingly, he lost, aided, as I have observed, by the usual manipulation of Hamas when a Labor Prime Minister of Israel is seeking re-election. One way to strengthen Israel's political institutions is to require that any party that is represented in the parliament or Knesset obtain at least 5 percent of the popular vote. This would cut the number of parties in parliament down to as few as three, instead of the ten or more that is currently quite normal.

After the attacks of September 11th, it may be that all manner of institutions of open government are under increased threat of manipulation, and that the material of the Middle East could acquire considerable relevance. Thus, the attack on the functioning of the democracy of India, apparently by Islamic militants, on the 13th December 2001 could be a worrying trend. It reminds me of the attack on British democracy by the Irish Republican Army, who blew up a large bomb in the hotel where the British prime minister and many of her ministers were staying during a party conference. Such attacks on democracy are open, and in one sense, easy to see, and in one sense, easy to defeat. By contrast, to catch sight of manipulation of the outcomes of elections, as I have argued has happened to Israel, is much more subtle. Most Israelis still seem not to have realized it. When Israelis do, it may help them avoid the blandishments of their Herut leaders. In general, manipulation of democratic institutions is one which could perhaps become a worldwide tendency after the attacks on America by Hamas' sister organization, Al Quaeda.

A Real Difference between Israelis and Palestinians

Inasmuch as I have been stressing culpable similarities between Israelis and Palestinians, it might be thought that I believed that it was all a matter of similarity between the two. In fact, there are some important differences. Israel no longer claims that the Arabs who left Israel in 1948 did so as a result of radio programs instructing them to leave. The reason that Israel no longer claims this is because Israeli historians like Benny Morris have been through the archives and shown what an unlikely fairy-tale story this is. For this to have occurred means that Israel had the honesty to allow him and other Israeli historians like Avi Shlaim who do not just accept whatever stories they have been told, but who attempt to base their beliefs about actual history on rigor. By contrast, I know of no such outbreak of concrete democratic honesty amongst the Palestinians, and if the American commentator, Edward Luttwak, is to be believed such honesty is extremely unlikely to occur whilst Mr. Arafat is still around. Thus, in an article in *Times Literary Supplement,* London, December 22, 2000, p. 12, Mr. Luttwak claimed that the following extraordinary incident occurred in 1998.

One of Mr. Arafat's friends wrote a piece comparing the struggle that Mr. Arafat has put up against Israel to that conducted by the famous Kurdish general, Salah al Din, who chased the Crusaders from Jerusalem and is normally known in the English speaking world as Saladin. The Arab newspaper, *Al Kuds,* published in East Jerusalem, had the piece on page three, not page one. Thereupon the editor was kidnapped by some of Mr. Arafat's men and physically assaulted at a secret venue for a week to allow him to understand that comparisons between Mr. Arafat and Salah al Din is material for page one, and not page three! When we compare the honesty of the Israeli authorities in allowing critical historians to comb Israel's archives with the incident of the *Al Kuds* editor, we see a striking difference between the two sides in terms of the protection of comforting political fairy tales. So, it is not the case that there are no differences between the two sides. Interestingly, surveys of opinion amongst young Palestinians have shown that over two-thirds of these admire the way Israeli democracy works for Israelis. Perhaps one good thing that could yet come out of all this is that the future Palestine may yet set a democratic example to the rest of the Arab world.

In conclusion, I think that I have demonstrated that a durable peace between Israel and the Palestinians would end not only a Clash of Civilizations, but a Clash of Symmetrizations. All in all, I think I have shown in this chapter that the Middle East offers to any student of symmetrization, "no end of lesson." Part of this "lesson" is that, once the kind of compromise, two-state peace is achieved, perhaps people may begin to reflect that ethnic community, far from being a nice simple good thing that alienated individualists represent it as being, always contains much collusive evasion of those truths about the community which that community's democratic deficits prevents being publicly confronted. Enthusiasts for community might use the material from the Israeli/Arab relationship to reflect on how fragile is the operation of that democracy by means of which it is sometimes possible, at least, to distinguish between the operation of community and the operation of a protection racket.

10

Other Symmetries of Political Life

I have given examples of the crucial role played by symmetrization in allowing Nazis and Communists to feel unbounded optimism in their support of their own projects, and unbounded loathing for those whom they took to be imperilling the future of humanity. For the Nazis, this last included the Jews and what the Nazis took to be "Jewish" teachings, whilst for the Communists, the target was the capitalist class and capitalism generally. I also demonstrated the importance of symmetrization in the situation in the Middle East.

I intend now to broaden my application of symmetrization to politics. To put two things into the same category is to say that these two things have something important in common, but this raises the question as to whether there are, in the world of politics, any privileged categories, or whether all categorizations of thought are more or less arbitrary expressions of power. Relativists would say the latter, and, in our day, this most often comes under the heading of post-modernism. Post-modernism seems to me to describe all categorizations as symmetrizations; all categorizations privilege some things as being important, and various other things are treated as less important and "pushed to the periphery" as the post-modernist expression goes. As an example, we may consider the Nazis, the Communists, and the liberals. The Nazis bracketed the Communists and the liberals together as people who opposed racialism, the Communists bracketed the Nazis and the liberals together as two outlooks which both accepted capitalism, certainly in practice, whilst the liberals bracketed the Nazis and the Communists together as two outlooks which were totalitarian. Well, history has given its own practical verdict, and it is the bracketing together of the Nazis and the Communists by the liberals which now seems the most crucial similarity, even though there were, of course, some differences, too, between the Nazis and the Communists. But the fondness for an utterly dominant state, for censorship and those sorts of similarities proved to have been the most crucial. In fact, the differences between these two proved not as great as either of them claimed. These sorts of points are around in contemporary debates. I'll consider several in turn.

Apartheid and Nazi Germany

The political—as distinct from the socio-economic—struggle against the apartheid policies of the old white government in South Africa ended in 1994 with the election of Nelson Mandela as the new post-apartheid president; the struggle had gone on since 1912 which had seen the formation of the African National Congress. The struggle had therefore taken eighty-two years. After 1945, it became common during the anti-apartheid struggle to bracket apartheid with Nazi Germany. Certainly, there were similarities between apartheid and what was unusual about Nazism:

1. Both had laws forbidding sex and marriage across certain ethnic lines; in Germany between "Aryans" and Jews, whilst in South Africa legislation recognized four race groupings, between whom sex and marriage were forbidden.
2. Both denounced liberalism; in Germany this was a "Jewish" outlook, whilst apartheid theorists described

83

this as a heathen teaching, because God allegedly split the races at the Tower of Babel.

3. Both apartheid and the Nazis engaged in detention in prison without trial, and the torture of detainees. Both regimes banned their respective Communist Parties.

4. After the Japanese attack on Pearl Harbor, the Nazis redefined the Japanese as "honorary Aryans" whilst as trade between Japan and apartheid blossomed in the 1960s, apartheid architect Dr. Verwoerd redefined the Japanese as "honorary whites."

5. This same architect of apartheid, Dr. Verwoerd, edited a newspaper during the Second World War in which he took a consistently anti-British stance. When another paper, *The Star,* wrote an editorial accusing Dr. Verwoerd of "speaking up for the Nazis," Dr. Verwoerd sued, but *The Star* was found not guilty of defamation of character. Dr. Verwoerd's successor as prime minister, Mr. Vorster, was detained for about eighteen months during the war for pro-Nazi activities. His brother, Mr. J.D. Vorster, was convicted in the Cape Town Supreme Court in 1941 of having attempted "to obtain information which would have been of use to an enemy," to quote the court's finding. This was information for the Nazi navy about the South African port of Simonstown, and he was sentenced to three years imprisonment. (Appellate Division 472, Cape Supreme Court 1941, Rex vs Vorster.)

This looks like a pretty damning list, and yet history showed that to equate apartheid with Nazism would have been a symmetrization. Thus there were also striking differences between the two systems. The most obvious was, firstly, the existence of opposition newspapers in South Africa, in which it was always possible to make fun of the apartheid government. Thus, when Dr. Verwoerd became prime minister in 1958, he announced that his new elevation had been the work of God. Thereupon, a cartoonist in a newspaper with a circulation in the tens of thousands showed Dr. Verwoerd seated at his desk one side of which supported a telephone whose handset Dr. Verwoerd was holding. But this telephone was no ordinary machine, for its cable went straight upwards through the ceiling to heaven where an angel was to be seen hovering and saying, "Hang on sir, I'll put you through." Whether it was Dr. Verwoerd who was being put through to God, or whether it was God who was being put through to Dr. Verwoerd was never made clear, but for the rest of Dr. Verwoerd's eight-year tenure as prime minister, cartoons of Dr. Verwoerd in this newspaper always included the trademark telephone with its cable going straight upwards through the ceiling. Although this may seem a trivial difference from Nazi Germany, where such a cartoon of any top Nazi would have been unthinkable, the fact was that this acceptance of the legitimate right of public criticism of the government eventually proved vital in allowing South Africa to dismantle apartheid and replace it with a non-racial democracy without going through a civil war. By contrast, no opposition in Germany was allowed and the Nazi regime went unchallenged until, at last, the armed might of the Soviet Union finally fought its way into Berlin. The ability of cartoonists to poke fun at the apartheid government largely punctured the symmetrizations which, unchallenged in Nazi Germany, produced fantasized infinities of racial potency. An excellent example of this was the Nazi film, *Triumph of the Will*; this is a clear example of an inauthentic infinity produced by symmetrization. By contrast, the apologists for apartheid had to make do with selective quotes from the Bible, which usage in turn was challenged by anti-apartheid Christians, and again, written up in opposition newspapers in South Africa.

So was apartheid South Africa *really* like Nazi Germany? Was it a case of predominant similarity with some differences, or was it more a case of predominant difference with some similarities? It seems to me that to look for some fixed, timeless answer across the whole society to this question is itself a symmetrization; to ask if *all* of the society was or was not predominantly like Nazi Germany is to try and ask a question about *all* of a society which can only be asked of this or that part. Broadly, I would say that apartheid society had neo-Nazi relations between the different races, but non-Nazi, non-totalitarian, multi-party politics. In the end, the multi-party political discipline triumphed in open democratic struggle—one much helped to its successful conclusion by economic sanctions by the rest of the world—and the Nazi social norms between ethnic groups declined. In other words, to declare that apartheid either was, or was not, like Nazi Germany is to abstract from history, from movement in time. Until the early 1970s, the similarities grew, but gradually the anti-apartheid struggle caused the similarities to decline and the differences to multiply.

So it is not merely a case of seeing differences in the context of similarities and similarities in the context of differences, but that these need not be fixed; they can be dynamic. Whilst similarities and differences between two systems never disappear, they can go in opposite directions; between 1948 and 1973, similarities between apartheid and Nazi Germany increased, and the differences decreased, but then, as happened under apartheid after 1973, when black trade unions managed to secure some important victories, similarities between apartheid and Nazism decreased and the differences increased. It took twenty-one years, from 1973 to 1994, and is an indication of the slowness with which these things can evolve. As someone who was a member of the anti-apartheid movement throughout this latter period, the evolution was often only apparent in retrospect.

Israel and Apartheid

A similar type of question to the above was being asked on the day of the September 11th attacks about Israel and apartheid—was Israel another apartheid South Africa, as Arabs tended to allege? Again we can certainly list some evident similarities:

a. Both South Africa's whites and Israeli Jews came to live in their respective lands as a result of imperialist presence of European powers—Holland and Britain in the case of South Africa, Britain chiefly in respect of Israel. For, in each case, it was the European power who decided that whites could emigrate to and settle in South Africa, and the British after 1918 who made the comparable decisions in respect of Jewish emigration to their then colony of Palestine.

b. The whites in South Africa had all the best jobs under apartheid, with blacks doing most of the heavy, dangerous, poorly paid work. Arabs tend to have this same role in Israel's economy.

c. Apartheid had some large disparities in the spending on the education of each white child and each black child. Something of this goes on in Israel, too, between Jews and Arabs.

d. Only whites in apartheid South Africa were conscripted into the army, whilst there were only a tiny number of mixed race or "colored" volunteers. In Israel, all Jews, both men and women, apart from students at Jewish religious schools, go to the army, but no Muslim Arabs are conscripted into it.

e. Whites in South Africa made much of being outnumbered by antagonistic blacks, and Israeli Jews feel the same way towards their Arab neighbors. The Holocaust performs much service here, and many Arabs have demonstrated the same mentality of the old Pan-Africanist Congress of South Africa, a black pride organization, under which South Africa's whites would not have found life very enjoyable, had they ever had to "enjoy" it.

f. Whites in South Africa seized all valuable mineral wealth, and Israelis have allocated eighty percent of the water of the area under Israeli control to Israel. This, in circumstances of semi-desert conditions.

Once again, we see numerous similarities between the two groups concerned. But then what of the differences? Arabs in Israel have, in theory, at least, the same rights as other Israelis, they vote for and stand as members of Israel's parliament, Arab families are not split up for fifty out of fifty-two weeks of most years, the way this used to happen under apartheid when blacks who went to work for whites were not allowed to bring their families with them. Where apartheid banned the South African Communist Party, Israel's equivalent, Rakach, has never been banned, whilst the one group that Israel has banned was the proto-fascist Jewish group, Kach, founded by Rabbi Meir Kahane. Kahane himself was banned from standing as a candidate for the Israeli parliament in 1984. Apartheid, by contrast, did not stop an ex-Nazi like Mr. Vorster who had not disavowed his Nazi past from becoming prime minister.

Again, as with apartheid and Nazi Germany, to say that Israel either is, or is not, another apartheid is fairly arbitrary; the less evasive question is: in which direction are changes moving? Towards more similarities and fewer differences between Israel and apartheid, or towards more differences and fewer similarities between Israel and apartheid? I'd say that when the Israeli Labor Party is in office, the differences between apartheid and Israel grow and the similarities decrease, but when the Herut is in power in Israel, the similarities with apartheid increase and the differences decrease.

Of course, the Palestinian group, Hamas, also supports apartheid, in that Islam's solution to the presence of Jews in an Islamic polity is like that of the Indians under apartheid, that of a protected minority. Everyone apart from the Herut/Hamas alliance, whose murderous operation I described in my chapter on the Middle East, knows that there is going to be a two-state solution, where Israel will broadly have to withdraw to the boundaries of May 1967, and Palestine will be an independent Arab state, a member of the Arab League, a member of the Organization of the Islamic Conference, etc. That solution has the potential at least to be seriously different from apartheid.

Saudi Arabia and Apartheid

I suggest that the state in the Middle East that most resembles old style apartheid is Saudi Arabia. Thus:

1. No pretense there of one person one vote, any more than apartheid did.
2. Consider the role played by Saudi oil in the world's economy compared to the role played by apartheid's exports of gold in the old days, too. It is very similar.
3. Apartheid employed millions of migratory workers who did all the most dangerous, most dirty and poorly paid work in the old apartheid economy. This is just what Saudi Arabia does today, where most of its migratory workers are other Muslims from Indonesia, Malaysia, and Pakistan. These "enjoy" about as much labor protection as apartheid used to show to its migratory black workers. Of course, there's no fuss about Saudi Arabia's migratory workers because these are fellow Muslims.
4. Saudi Arabia is more Juden-frei, i.e. free of Jews, than Nazi Germany ever managed; in fact, no Jew may live

there. The constitution of Saudi Arabia only allows Muslims to pray there.

5. Whereas post-1948, apartheid actually frowned on expressions of Nazi attitudes to Jews, we see the open circulation in Saudi Arabia of the old Nazi Protocols of the Elders of Zion beliefs about the World Jewish Conspiracy. Thus, some twelve weeks after the attacks of September 11th, the Saudi government daily paper *al-Watan* ran two articles repeating all the usual Elders of Zion make-believe. (See MEMRI, December 28th 2001.)

One difference between apartheid and Saudi Arabia is that apartheid was more liberal than Saudi Arabia. I happen to have had personal experience with this. Thus, I once spent a whole afternoon discussing atheism in the old apartheid South Africa with a Mrs. Winnifred Roux, by then a very elderly member of the old South African Rationalist Society, which had existed then for about thirty years. In the course of the discussion, she openly gave me a copy of Bertrand Russell's pamphlet "Why I am not a Christian" to read. Also, apartheid prided itself on being based on what Afrikaans supporters of apartheid used to call Christian Nationalism. By contrast, I've yet to hear of a Rationalist Society in Riyadh, and it would probably not be a good idea to try and establish one for thirty minutes, let alone thirty years.

So people who want, therefore, to compare Israel and apartheid should, if they are Muslims, bear in mind Saudi Arabia's greater closeness to apartheid, and indeed in some ways Nazism. Nor do I see the similarities between apartheid and Saudi Arabia decreasing and differences increasing. These seem to be fairly static so far.

I note from all of the above cases, ultimately, no two situations are wholly different or exactly alike. Humans are just neither that similar to each other, nor that different from each other. It is difference in the context of similarity, and similarity in a context of difference. Yet, despite this, not all political systems are of equal value. Liberal democracy is the type of government in which the fake infinities that arise from symmetrization have the greatest chance of being exposed as being of a fantasized nature. Note, I say the greatest chance, not that the chance is itself great, at least in the short to medium term. That is why open public criticism of all beliefs relating to public matters is so vital. It is why democracy is not just "a point of view" or one system amongst many equally valid systems. Liberal multi-party democracy has the great virtue of being that system in which the inauthentic infinities have the greatest chance of being exposed as abstractions from whatever was thinkable at the time that the holy books were assembled. The Qu'ran, for example, was assembled in about the Christians' seventh century, so when Islamic militants cry "Allah is the Way" the arguments of this book suggest that a more authentic version of the claim would be "Seventh Century Abstraction is the Way." For, although religion can sometimes survive unchallenged amongst some sections of the population of an urbanized liberal democracy, nevertheless it is from just this kind of society where the infinities involved in religious belief are most likely to be queried and ignored; and none more, perhaps, than that religion's moral teachings. I'll look at more of this in the concluding chapter to this book.

III
The Economic Context of Terrorism

Introduction

This book so far has explored a particular way of thinking, a way which produces falsities that many people have found seductive. But just what particular way of thinking dominates politically, and, in particular, captures state power, can depend very strongly on economic developments. Thus, although the Great Depression of the 1930s did not cause the thinking of the Nazi Party, it was that economic development that catapulted the Nazi Party into state power. The worst of the economic downturn of those years began in late 1929, reached its worst in June 1932, and then improved. The percentage of the German electorate which voted for the Nazis followed these economic contours extremely closely. We can see this from Snyder (*Encyclopaedia of the Third Reich,* McGraw Hill, 1976, front matter). In the elections for the central parliament on May 20th 1928 the Nazis obtained 2.5 percent of the votes cast, but 18 percent on September 14th 1930, and up to a maximum of 42 percent on July 31st 1932 but then declined to 37 percent on 6th of November 1932. Thereafter, the climb into state power of the Nazis occurred as a result of political twists and turns. In the right circumstances, something like this could repeat itself and catapult organizations of religious militants into state power. This could cause a large disaster were this to occur in any large and economically important country, or in one which had the atom bomb, or in a substantial number of smaller countries. On the day of the attacks in New York and Washington, Islamic militants were already holding state power in Iran and in the Sudan, and showed no sign of being dislodged. Accordingly, I am going to be interested in looking in this chapter and the two that follow it at the economic dimensions of our post September 11th situation.

One point needs to be made early on. The country which the terrorists of September 11th attacked is often called a "developed" country, in contradistinction to the sort of country from which the attackers came, namely a "developing" country. This language seems to me a mixture of insult and complacency: thus I take "developed" to be an immensely complacent term, as if the so-called developed countries have no need of any further evolution, as if everything in them was already so advanced and indeed developed! "Developing" does make some sense as an economic term, but I think it misses one of the main features of the post-September 11th world, which is that the urbanized way of life is becoming the universal norm of human life. Here is, I think, the reality behind many of the cries about the worldwide loss of cultural diversity, of "American cultural colonialism" and the like. The fact that forms of urbanization are becoming the human norm also has large implications for the depth and extent of religious belief, an apparently important factor for the attackers of September 11th, who seem to have felt that their version of this was being assaulted. So, in place of "developing" and "developed" way of life, I think that the fact of rapid urbanization needs to be continually kept in mind and to help do this I will distinguish the *urbanized* countries from the *urbanizing* countries. The urbanized countries are of course those in which liberal capitalism is the most securely established; one could not have said this prior to the demise of the Soviet bloc but it is one part of the truth of our post-Soviet times. Since it is liberal capitalism and the transition to more individualist norms that religious militants oppose, my first task in opposing them must be to show that liberal capitalism, far from being the satanic force that they and some anti-globalization and environmental protesters paint it as, makes vital contributions to the solution of the problems of our modern condition. This is what I shall now do.

11

What Liberal Capitalism Contributes to the World

As I've already noted, the people who carried out the attacks of September 11th were not great fans of liberal democracy and its capitalist context. So far as the relation between liberal capitalism and other forms of society goes, the following quote from Karl Marx's *Theories of Surplus Value,* Lawrence and Wishart, 1969, Volume 2, Page 118, seems to be relevant:

> . . . although, at first, the development of the capacities of the human species takes place at the cost of the majority of human individuals and even classes, in the end, it breaks through this contradiction and coincides with the development of the individual; the higher development of individuality is thus only achieved by a historical process during which individuals are sacrificed for the interests of the species in the human kingdom, as in the plant and animal kingdoms, always assert themselves at the cost of the interests of individuals, because these interests of the species coincide only with the interests of certain individuals, and it is this coincidence which constitutes the strength of these privileged individuals.

I think that in these post Soviet times, it is the leaderships of liberal capitalism that most often have the justified privilege of which the piece speaks. This is my main claim, and had the attackers of September 11th heard it, they would have undoubtedly disputed it. For this reason, since people of their commitment to their ideas could be around for another hundred years, we'd better have some unusually rigorous grounds to dispute with them.

Well then, in what sense do the "interests of the species" coincide at least 51 percent with the interests of liberal capitalism? I will give two kinds of answers; the first will be materialist and the other will be some brief thoughts about questions of spirituality, and the much discussed "God-sized hole" in liberal capitalist life. I'll then look at something else capitalism has a tendency to produce, which is the destruction of all barriers to trade, in the name of globalization.

Firstly, some problems of a scientific type and what liberal capitalism contributes to their solution:

Problem One—The Warming of the Earth

Average temperatures on Earth have warmed by about 0.6 degrees centigrade in the hundred years prior to September 11th and, increasingly, it is becoming possible to understand, via the concept of the greenhouse gas, the contribution to this warming being made by humans. This concept of the greenhouse gas was first developed in the United States in 1985. There is only one realistic way to stop human beings from pouring the main greenhouse gas, carbon dioxide, into the atmosphere in ever greater and greater amounts and that is to develop forms of minimally polluting renewable energy to replace power generation by fossil fuels. In this regard the (American) website *www.windustry.com* records how the cost of generating one kilowatt hour of energy by wind had, in the thirty years before September 11th, come down from the fifty cents to four cents. But on September 11th, to generate electricity by burning coal still cost just two cents a kilowatt hour. So, although there is still some way to go, there had been massive progress. Certainly, the only serious way to reduce the human contribution to the warming of the earth is to cut greenhouse gas emission, and this can only be done by providing cheap electricity via renewables. I will show in Chapter 14 that this has another crucial link to the development of liberal capitalism which seems so far unknown and which it is an aim of this book to explain and illustrate.

Talking about methods of generating heat and power, we may note how societies *other than* those of liberal capitalism have encouraged the spread of deserts over the centuries; thus the Sahara Desert has only existed for some 8000 years and it seems likely that societies that lack the science and productivity of liberal capitalism were forced to destroy all trees in their desperate search for heat, something which still continues on a destructively large scale in some pre-industrial countries to this day. So much for the reality—as compared to the image—of what the nature enhancing effects of a pre-industrial and pre-capitalist way of life can be like. There is also the fact that many greenhouse gas emissions come not from industry but from emissions of methane from farm animals, such as pigs. This must have been making a contribution to keeping up the temperature over all of human history, but now due to the science developed under liberal capitalism, we have an understanding of this process which is universally true throughout the whole world and over all time. Indeed, it may be that to further reduce the rate of global warming we may have to have far fewer farm animals, and that humanity, in addition to other measures, will also have to become much more vegetarian! Whatever the outcome of this, though, it is the rigorous, and apparently unarguable understanding of the greenhouse gas which has been developed in liberal capitalism which is powering the determination to reduce greenhouse gas emission; the only question is which is the best, most cost-effective way, for the technology developed by liberal capitalism to tackle this.

Problem Two—Pollution

If liberal capitalism really is poisoning the world, this is something that would be especially difficult to hush up. Certainly, if there is a serious risk of this, the tools of science which liberal capitalism has done so much to develop would be likely to warn us in time. This has already happened once over aerosols and other chlorofluorocarbons and the damage they do to the ozone layer. Thus, enough action has apparently been taken for us to be able to look forward to the ozone layer replenishing itself by mid twenty-first century. Acid rain has also been reduced, again due to a mixture of the rigor of science, which has so developed in the three hundred years of liberal capitalism, and liberal democratic pressurizing of politicians.

Problem Three—Extinction of Biological Species

There seems to be widespread agreement amongst people who study the extinction of biological species that there was a large amount of destruction in the hundred years before the attacks of September 11th. There clearly needs to be more democratic pressure to reduce this, although it is also worth noting that our present round of mass extinctions is the sixth mass extinction, as this has occurred five times before: the Ordovician, 430 million years ago, the Devonian, 350 million years ago, the Permian, 225 million years ago, the Triassic, 200 million years ago, and the Cretacious, 65 million years ago. Our present round of destruction may thus be the sixth such. I do not mention the previous five to breed complacency, but to point out that the idea that what is now alive is some indigenous, never-to-be-recreated life-forms, is false. If evolution is true, new species will continue to evolve. Thus, although humanity would be stupid not to try and save what we can, since for one thing we don't even know what we are losing, the idea that liberal capitalism is some uniquely destructive force of our environment is false. On the contrary, liberal capitalist technology will probably enable us to prevent further mass destruction by collision of our earth with a large meteorite, as apparently caused the mass extinction of sixty-five million years ago.

Problem Four—AIDS

On September 11th, it was less than twenty years since the cause of AIDS was understood, yet there already were new drugs available which either slowed up the development of full-blown AIDS in someone who was already HIV positive, or which greatly reduced the chance of an HIV positive mother passing on the virus to her unborn child. By contrast, if we take the plague that ravaged Europe for over three hundred years, no one had the faintest understanding of where it came from or what to do about it. At the time, the Jews were blamed and frequently expelled from towns and cities, ten thousand people mainly women were killed, often hideously by burning, under the allegation of witchcraft in the general crisis that seized the nations of Europe. Compare this with the fact that once the new syndrome of AIDS had been recognized in 1980, the understanding of its cause, HIV, had been worked up within three short years. From this, it promptly became possible to understand how AIDS is transmitted, namely from one human to another via body fluids such as blood and semen. No blaming of Jews and pogroms against them this time or the burning of women, and even the attempts to call AIDS the "gay-plague" didn't cause liberal society to attack the newly won freedoms of gay people either. Quite the reverse; once it was understood that gay people were especially vulnerable, some extra resources have been made available to this community. Twenty years after AIDS had been recognized, there were treatments to slow down its spread and billions of dollars were being spent trying to find a vaccine. The work towards a possible antidote to AIDS would be nowhere without the huge resources poured into it by liberal capitalism. Already over twenty million people have died of AIDS and over thirty-six million are infected, according to the United States-based anti-AIDS website, *www.fightaidsathome.org.*

Meanwhile, the science developed under liberal capitalism has enabled chemists to investigate the curative possibilities of various chemicals in a mathematical way on home computers. At the end of the year of the September 11th attacks, the *www.fightaidsathome.org* site had over 40,000 such home computers working for it which had contributed over six million hours of computer time and allowed the completion of some three million tasks. All this time was given freely—which somewhat contradicts the idea that under liberal capitalism people only do things for a stranger if there is a cash payment. The majority of strangers who will benefit most from all this are in the urbanizing countries of Africa and Asia, who are currently suffering for the lack of better drugs to fight AIDS.

A further complication is that mutations by the HIV virus make those drugs that have been developed less effective. To overcome this, therefore, requires a continuous research effort, and what system other than liberal capitalism can even conceive of providing this? In this regard, it is remarkable it seems to me, that for all the talk by the old Soviet state about taking the side of the "toiling masses," the Soviet Union seems to have played a zero, or next to zero, role in developing new vaccines, despite having trained up a huge cadre of scientists. Only liberal capitalism, which has liberal democracy as its political form seems able to produce the openness compatible with the sort of creative effort required for such a task.

Now, one undoubted problem of producing drugs as commodities, as is inevitable under capitalism, is the question of producing them at a price that most people who most need those drugs can afford. This problem, however, is being attended to; thus

Brazil has managed to cut its deaths from AIDS by 40 percent in the 1990s. Partly this has been due to the copying of the original drugs by other drug companies which are themselves based in the urbanizing countries, such as India; and by hook or by crook, the people who most need the drugs are slowly getting them. Some of the governments of the urbanizing countries, like the one headed by post-apartheid President, Thabo Mbeki, of South Africa, have been a bigger obstacle to reducing the spread of AIDS than all the pricing policies of all the drug companies put together. But crucially, without the huge productive capacities of the drug firms, I question whether these drugs would even exist to be copied, or to be even argued about by health professionals.

In this regard, it's well worth noting that it was the United States that produced penicillin on such a vast industrial scale that there's enough in the world for *all* of humanity and available often even to the poorest people. In Baxter (*Scientists Against Time,* Little Brown 1946, MIT Press, 1968, pages 337 to 359), there is a brief account of the enormous and wholly successful effort by the United States—over some three and a half wartime years from the summer of 1941 until March 1945—to mass produce penicillin in vast enough quantities for their soldiers on the front. As a result, it has become freely available to all of humanity; even in 1945 it was being sold at such a low price that it was soon being used worldwide. These extraordinary pages in Baxter should be compulsory reading by those ignoramuses who think of, or refer to, the United States as the Great Satan!

Problem Five—Cancer Control

In 1971, American President Richard Nixon persuaded Congress to set up the National Cancer Institute within the National Institute of Health to specifically devote funds for cancer research. By the 1990s, this had a budget exceeding two billion dollars annually (Robert N. Proctor in the *Oxford Companion to United States History,* ed. Paul Boyer, Oxford University Press, 2001, page 102). No country can currently compete with the center of liberal capitalism for mobilizing funds for research from which all peoples benefit, and the chemistry department at Oxford University in England is using some half a million personal computers via the internet to investigate some 3.5 billion molecules for possible new therapies against cancer. They estimate that they will need ninety million hours of number crunching to run a preliminary check on all these molecules. It is via its website *www.ud.com* that they do this. Only capitalism could seriously imagine setting up a worldwide network to fight a major scourge of humanity—again where was the old Soviet Union and its friends in the Warsaw Pact in relation to cancer research? Although it is true that the biggest *proportion* of those who die of cancer are those of the urbanized countries, nevertheless the *numbers* of deaths from cancer in the urbanizing countries are not inconsiderable either.

A step forward will occur when each web browser allows an option to allow their user to easily and automatically connect that personal computer to the health website of his or her choice, and make a massive and unprecedented contribution via computational chemistry to health care.

Problem Six—Keeping Skilled Scientists in the Urbanizing Countries

One criticism of the urbanized liberal capitalist countries is that they have been enticing away the most educated people of the urbanizing countries with higher wages, better research facilities, etc. One good consequence of the internet is that it is now a lot easier for a laboratory in an urbanizing country to stay up-to-date with the very latest research results. This should help keep a larger percentage of the highly-educated people from emigrating to the urbanized countries. The internet would, of course, be quite unthinkable without liberal capitalism's massive encouragement of science.

It's also worth adding at this point how misconceived have been the attacks on what is portrayed as elite science, carried on for a tiny, wealthy, mainly white minority, whilst the mainly black poor of the world still suffer from well known killer diseases for which there were still no vaccines on September 11th. Thus, I can recall the night of the 2nd December 1967, when Professor Chris Barnard carried out his first heart transplant operation in Cape Town, during the bad old days of apartheid. Now, it was said—rightly—that less than a kilometer from where Dr. Barnard did his transplants, black children starved for the lack of a bottle of milk a day. But the biggest problem with heart transplants was rejection of the donor organ by the recipient's immune system. This, in turn, stimulated research on the immune system, and then, less than fifteen years later, we suddenly hit HIV/AIDS, which kills because it allows opportunistic infections to overwhelm the body's immune system. Overnight, then, this increased research on the immune system due to the heart transplant stimulus became immensely valuable, and for some thirty-six million people, many of them amongst the world's poorest, who were HIV positive on September 11th.

Problem Seven—Spiritual Matters

Whether life has any unchanging universal meaning is something that has been hotly debated for centuries. Liberal capitalism is often seen by its critics, especially its religious critics, as being an especially empty form of life. However, in the light of Chapter 5, which shows how the infinities of religion show grave signs of deriving from symmetrization, the question arises whether this perceived spiritual emptiness of liberal capitalism doesn't derive from a form of society in which inauthentic infinities of religion *are most seen through and justly disbelieved,* and thus ignored by and large (except at the three well known ceremonial points in life, namely hatch, match and dispatch). Here are three events which produce infinities of feeling that really are authentic!

Although it seems impossible to derive any morality from studying the universe, cosmology is the science of this search and this science is most encouraged under liberal capitalism. It may not be as comforting as the infinities of religion, but if my discussion of previous chapters is anything to go by, people under liberal capitalism are those most confronting the truths of human existence with the least number of fairy tales. This is not something which I think is likely to have occurred to the attackers of September 11th.

Now, I am going to turn from areas where I think the record of liberal capitalism is at its most positive to a more ambivalent question. The question of trade barriers is a major question of contemporary liberal capitalism, and as this form of society is most frequently led by the United States, I am going to look at a brief history of American trade barriers. As these have been very large in the past, I think America does owe the rest of the world an explanation as to why they were right to develop tariff barriers in the past, but to oppose the existence of trade barriers now.

A Brief History of American Trade Barriers

The United States is arguably the world's largest producer and exporter of finished goods, which is how a country becomes affluent and respected. Since 1947, it has lectured the rest of the world about the virtues of free trade. Yet, the United States itself became the vast producer and exporter of finished goods that it did from behind extremely heavy trade barriers. The first tariffs levied by Americans go back to 1787 when an assembly of the thirteen colonies who had won the War of Independence with Britain met in New York. This assembly levied tariffs partly to protect infant American industries and partly to raise revenue. These tariffs were raised after the invasion of the United States by Britain between 1812–1814. Later still, when war again returned to the United States in the form of the American Civil War which broke out in 1861, and representatives from the southern states ceased to attend debates in Congress and vote on new legislation, the northern States promptly raised protection of the infant industries, most of which were in the North, by setting a tariff of 48 percent on many imported goods; this was the Morill Tariff Act of 1861. For the next eighty years, the greatest supporters of ever higher tariffs in the United States were the Republicans, something that only changed in the 1940s.

Nor were all acts which raised tariffs in the United States simply passed and then forgotten about, for tariff policies of successive governments in the United States were a matter of huge and ongoing public discussion. To mention but one such instance, in the presidential elections of 1888, the maintenance of tariffs was the major plank in the campaign, and a new tariff act of 1890 raised tariffs still further. The measure was put through by a man named William McKinley, and it did his political future no harm, for he shortly thereafter became (Republican) President himself in 1896. The act from 1890 was then followed by the Dingley Tariff Act of 1897 which raised tariffs to record levels, followed by yet further tariff increases under the Payne-Aldrich Act of 1909. In 1913, the tariff was lowered to 25 percent at the instigation of Democrat President Woodrow Wilson, only to be raised again in 1921, 1922 and 1930 when the Republicans were again in power. Thereafter, the tariff from 1930 remained broadly intact until 1947, when a Democrat American administration set up the General Agreement on Tariffs and Trade (GATT) to cut tariffs worldwide. (Details in this section from *The Limits of Liberty,* Maldwin A. Jones, Oxford University Press, 1996.)

It seems a fair question since the setting up of the World Trade Organization in 1995, again with the strongest American commitment: would its rules allow any country to copy Uncle Sam and protect infant industries with tariffs of 48 percent whilst still being able to export the way the United States was still able to continue to export after the end of the American Civil War in 1865? If not, is the United States preventing countries from producing and exporting finished goods using America's own tried and tested method of tariff protection and thus helping to maintain world poverty amongst the world's urbanizing countries?

This last possibility seems to me only to hold if the rate at which the urbanizing countries were able to produce and export goods, especially finished goods, declined compared to what would have been the case had trade barriers remained or even grown.

Such questions are extremely hard to test not least because of the cyclical movement of economic growth. I will look at this further in the next chapter.

One objection to the global spread of commodity production to all of humanity is that this will reduce the diversity of cultures that currently exist. No doubt, some reduction in cultural diversity is indeed inevitable but it's odd to be mourning this when liberal capitalism is also regularly criticized for allegedly not helping other countries to develop. Culturally, this would seem to mean that the liberal capitalist countries are being criticized for not helping other countries enough to become like them, that is to acquire more of modern science and the capitalist can-do culture.

Now, I do not see that a policy of developing one's own domestic industry behind tariff barriers has always worked so well; thus, it seems in general not to have encouraged large industrial development of South America, even though policies of protective tariffs operated throughout that region for over a century. The United States industrialized behind trade barriers that lasted for over a hundred and fifty years, Japan and the so-called "Tiger" economies of Southeast Asia have managed something similar, but a policy of protective tariffs seems to be no simple panacea. Meanwhile—and this is entirely new for the United States—as a result of having lowered trade barriers, the United States has become the world's *importer of last resort.* That's a point of considerable importance—to have the world's biggest and wealthiest economy open to the *exports* of all the world's other nations, including its urbanizing economies which often need new markets to develop.

All in all then, the main beneficial contribution of liberal capitalism is predominantly in the vital area of new commodities that make the biggest contribution in the reduction of human suffering due to ignorance, but that its main negative tendency may now be that it attacks the use by others of the tariff methods that, for example, the United States itself used to give its infant industries a chance to become competitive.

The spread of capitalism is making the demographic pattern of the urbanized countries universal:

> From a pattern of high death rates and high birth rates to one of low death rates and low birth rates . . . mortality rates usually start to decline before the fall in birth rates. In the interim, populations expand substantially until smaller numbers of children become the norm. Hence the population explosion in the short term. (*One World Divisible,* David Reynolds, Penguin 2000, p 137.)

If the logic I have argued out is accepted, then this means that progress by humanity depends on the spread of capitalism, and that in this regard, support for the pre-capitalist aspects of religions, like the heavy restrictions on interest, really are reactionary. Thus to the extent that religious militants are anti-capitalist, it is Marx's arguments, such as we saw in the quote with which we began this chapter, that are the best arguments why capitalism and forms of economic globalization are most worthy of support. It would be easy to work this position up into a satire: to say that the main culpable contribution of the most religious militants is not to recognize that, because liberal capitalism accumulates capital so brilliantly, the interests of the human species more nearly coincide with the commodity producing interests of liberal capitalism than anything else, and if only religious types weren't such pre-Marxist ignoramuses, they would recognize this. So, really, the scores of branches of the British Council, the United States Information Service and similar bodies overseas ought, on this account, to run courses in the local languages that this most productive culture of liberal capitalism is the only sensible thing to support. For inasmuch as capitalism has out-produced every other kind of culture that has so far existed, these pre-capitalist features of other cultures will eventually exist only in history or on the stage.

12

The Probability of Globalized Growth in Long-Term Destitution

Introduction

I argued in the introduction to Part III, which began my discussion of the economics, that a long slowdown in economic growth could be a very serious development in the struggle against terrorism. As a result, if there were reasons to expect such a long period during which overall economic growth was likely to be unreliable and if the onset of such a period could be predicted with any confidence, then this information would be well worth having. This is the task of this chapter. In it, I shall present evidence that since the 1820s there have been long waves of overall growth of the capitalist economies as a whole which last a total of about fifty years. These divide into two cycles which broadly consist of:

a. Periods during which overall economic expansion occurred regularly and reliably, but which was punctuated by more or less short periods of little or no growth.
b. Periods in which overall economic expansion was irregular and unreliable, but which were punctuated by more or less short periods of good growth.

These long waves have been longest for the economies of Europe since the 1820s, although the United States has tended to join them since 1929. I will first give a table which summarizes the main long-wave movements.

Table 12.1 Summary of the Long-Wave Cycle I Am Going to Argue for

1826–1848	Generally low overall growth period in Europe
1848–1873	Major years of overall growth in the nineteenth century in Europe
1873–1896	More hesitant overall growth with agriculture in special difficulty
1896–1921	Predominantly a good overall growth period
1921–1948	Low overall growth starts in Europe; slump after 1929 in all of capitalism
1948–1973	Golden years of the twentieth century capitalist growth, worldwide
1973–1996	More difficult period with only hesitant overall growth

Why these waves have this marked duration of about fifty years for one complete cycle remains a mystery; it is discussed but not solved in a large book of 687 pages titled *Long Wave Theory* by C. Freeman (ed.), Edward Elgar, 1996. However, we shall see that the waves have shown remarkable constancy, regardless of many political happenings, so that the continuation of these long waves into the future shows every sign of being the best guess about the future of world economic growth, unless upset by world war or a large civil war, such as the American Civil War, which are about the only things that have so far upset these waves.

I will now present some simple charts to support my claim that there are long waves of economic growth as shown in Table 12.1. The important thing is to compare the charts, and to look particularly at their overall shape. This process of comparing is made easier because for all the graphs the horizontal axis is always go-

Chart 1
Annual Compound Rates of Growth in World Trade
(at Constant Prices 1820–1967)

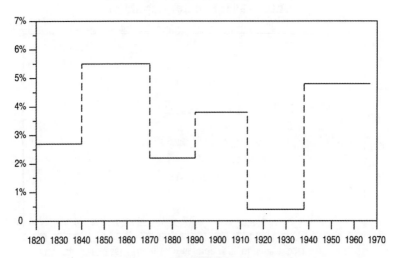

Chart 2
Annual Compound Rate of Growth of
Industrial Output in Britain (1827–1967)

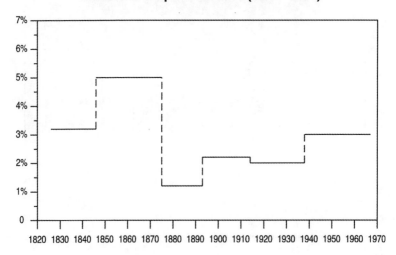

Chart 3
Annual Compound Rates of Growth of Industrial Output in Germany
(After 1945: Federal Republic)

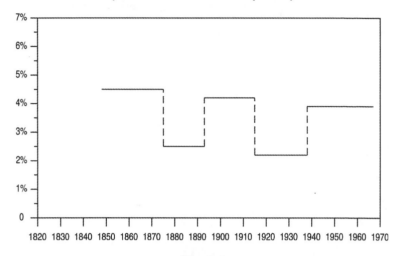

Chart 4
Annual Growth in World Output of Energy

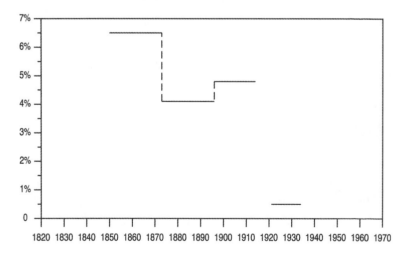

Chart 5
Indexes of Per Capita World Production

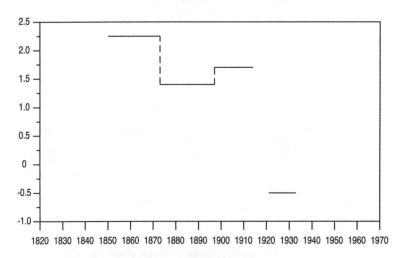

Chart 6
Short Term Interest Rates (Decimal Averages)
Britain

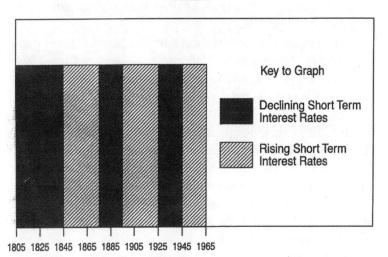

Key to Graph

Declining Short Term
Interest Rates

Rising Short Term
Interest Rates

Chart 7
World (I) Industrial Production
(1780–1979)

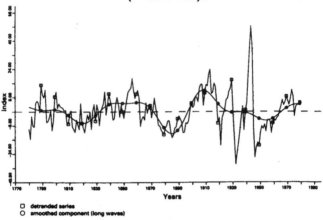

World (I) industrial production 1780–1979

ing to be years from 1820 to about 1970. Each vertical axis is a rate of growth of some item.

The graphs were drawn from tables in Mandel, *Long Waves of Capitalist Development,* Cambridge University Press, 1980, Verso 1995, pgs, 3, 4, and 15.

When we look at the first three charts, namely 1, 2, and 3, the resemblance in their shapes is striking, and ties up with the claims of Table 12.1. This is especially interesting in that the charts are about three somewhat different things; the first records changes in world trade, the second records industrial output in Britain, and the third records industrial output by Germany.

The next two charts, numbers 4 and 5, are for shorter periods of time than the previous three, they still show the same shape, one broadly consistent with Table 12.1. Accordingly, they are further evidence for the claim of the long waves claimed in the table.

The first five charts suggest that years like 1848, 1873, 1896, 1921, 1948 are crucial watershed years. To further add to the evidence that these really were watershed years, marking the beginnings and ends of phases of the long waves, I will now turn to looking at Chart 6 of interest rates. Now, if economic growth is good and regular, interest rates will tend to rise, whereas if economic growth is lower or more irregular, interest rates will tend to fall. The sixth chart simply distinguishes between periods when interest rates are rising and when they are declining. This is a chart for British interest rates and from the early nineteenth century until 1945, Britain was a very important trading center. So, the fact that British interest rates go through phases of between twenty years to thirty years during which they are either continually rising or continually falling is especially significant. It is a very important reflection of long-wave behavior. Also, note the years in which the changeovers occur, namely at the boundaries of the bars. These are at 1845, 1875, 1895, 1925 and 1945, which although it doesn't fit the table 12.1 perfectly, it nevertheless fits very closely.

I will now add just one further chart, Chart 7, that of world industrial production; again, the wave shape is unmistakable.

It is taken from Rainer Metz, *A Re-examination of Long Waves in Aggregate Production Series,* and quoted in C. Freeman, *Long Wave Theory,* Edward Elgar, 1996, p. 506.

I would summarize all this by saying that we see the same broad pattern, especially for European economies, with the United States tending to join these patterns after 1873, and even more often, after 1929. With this caveat, the measures broadly support the pattern argued for in my first table, Table 12.1. This is surely striking since the measures quoted differ from each other.

In thinking about these phases of the long waves, one must think in terms of the predominant economic weight of the world, and not expect each and every economy to obediently march in step at all points and on all dates. Thus, Japan of the 1990s was in recession pretty well all the time, and Germany had to pay for re-unification of the old West and East Germany, so neither of these exactly followed the transition to predominant expansion which however was plainly evident throughout much of the capitalist world by the mid 1990s. Other countries, like China and Russia, will also take time to predominantly join the long-wave cycle, because a country which is still industrializing very fast, as the United States was particularly before 1873, will not join the cycle until its economy has developed to quite a high fraction of its maximum potential. Obviously, something local, big and unusual, such as the Civil War in the United States, 1861–1865, will have local effects of an unpredictable kind.

To these charts we can add a further consideration. If we think of a complete wave as being about fifty years in duration, and as fifty divides into a hundred, we would expect some similarity in the behavior of the European and the other economies of the urbanized countries, every one hundred years. In this regard:

a. The years of 1873 and 1973 are both years in which there is a transition from a period of growth to a broadly non-expansionary period. The mid-1890s and the mid-1990s both saw the reverse of this, when there was a transition to a period of good growth from what had, in each case, been a broadly non-expansionary period.

b. The 1840s in England were described as the "hungry forties" and the 1930s were as well. This is not exactly a gap of one hundred years, but the repetition is striking nevertheless.

c. The capitalist boom from 1848–1873 in much of Europe resembles strikingly the boom of 1948–1973, although the absolute levels of prosperity were of course several times greater in the latter twenty-five-year period. But there is a striking similarity in the nature of the two twenty-five year periods, separated by a hundred years.

d. The period of 1873–1896 shows marked economic similarities to the period 1973 to 1996.

Except for the years 1973–1996, I think I have given enough data to broadly support the claims of my first table, Table 12.1. The worst downturn evidently occurred in the 1930s, and just why that one was so bad is still argued by economists. One factor was evidently the enormous wastage of the First World War, in which investment for the four years, 1914–1918, was poured into armaments, but spending on these had few peacetime uses. In this, there was to be significant difference from the Second World War, in which as we shall see in a later chapter, investments in the war effort made for a number of new commodities after 1945, which made for considerable new employment opportunities.

Reflection on the Stability of the Long-Wave Patterns

I want to reflect on the remarkable stability of the long wave patterns. Thus, apart from the two world wars, none of the other actions engaged in by many politicians of many stripes, by trade union behavior, by the Russian Revolution of 1917, nor its ultimate demise in 1991, or even the larger Chinese one of 1949, nor the facts of the cold war, seem to have fundamentally altered the shape of these waves, to have had more than a marginal effect on the lengths of the cycles, etc. Whatever causes these waves of capitalist fluctuation, the result seems to me to be broadly and extraordinarily predictable.

It might be thought that globalization might alter the expected behavior of these waves. However, amidst all the talk about how this is opening up economies to each other in an unprecedented way, Paul Hirst and Grahame Thompson (in *Globalization in Question, Polity, Second Edition,* 1999), present all manner of measures to argue that the World Trade Organization's rules have mainly re-established the levels of trade that the most advanced countries of the world enjoyed with each other in 1913, before the First World War. This last increased barriers of various kinds and it was from these and their descendants that the world has been moving away from since 1947. Yet, despite all the different mixes of free trade and hindrances to free trade that have been practiced since the 1820s when the data of my table begins, the waves go on with their familiar shape and duration.

Why These Waves Are So Little Known

It is striking if one reads the work of economic historians how relatively little these waves are referred to. This is a large subject, but one reason that these waves have had relatively little airing is because they bear little resemblance to movements of stock exchange share prices. Also, prices of ordinary commodities don't always show similar movements to these long waves: thus the price of computers continues to plummet as per Moore's Law, which says that the price of a computer halves every eighteen months, but this has been going on for about twenty years, regardless of the long wave. It could also be that during the Cold War, the supporters of capitalism were not keen to advertise the fact that the system had definite patterns of uncertain and irregular overall growth.

Expectation about the Future after September 11th

The patterns we have studied in this chapter can lead us to expect that neither globalization, nor increased urbanization, nor the accession of China, India and Russia to the World Trade Organization, nor the demise of the socialist and communist movements and the ending of the capitalist versus Marxist cold war are singly or jointly likely to make any serious difference to the prediction of a continuation of this long wave cycle. We can thus expect the world economy at the beginning of the twenty-first century to be in another twenty to twenty-five year long phase, one of predominant expansion. Since this began in the early to mid 1990s, we can expect this phase to continue to between 2015–2020. *By 2020, we should expect the transition to a period of irregular and uncertain overall growth.*

If such a transition can be expected towards the end of the second decade of our new century, the other obvious question is how serious, generally, can we expect the next phase to be? It might seem that it would be a hopeless task to try and predict, but I think that one fact makes it likely that the twenty-five year period after 2020 may well be an unusually serious one socially. This is obviously that in our post-September 11th world, an unusually severe growth in poverty carries with it the possibility of helping to recruit large numbers of people for religious militancy and terrorism. I will now turn to the next chapter to discuss how serious the next downturn could well be.

13

What the Next Unreliable Growth Phase Could Be Like

One of the things that did most to aid the growth of the old Communist parties was the growth of destitution of the 1930s. If anything even fairly similar were to recur, this would greatly reduce the attractiveness to hundreds of millions of people of capitalist globalization and would do much to encourage religious militants. This might be especially likely amongst angry people from the world's 1.2 billion Muslims because Muslims are so spread out across the world: thus, about one-quarter of the states in the world are members of the Organization of the Islamic Conference. By contrast, whilst a similar number of Hindus to Muslims may well be poor and newly urbanized, Hindus are concentrated mainly in the single state of India. I will argue that this makes Muslims much more likely to be involved in disputes, which, however, may be no more of their own particular making than those between, say, Hindus and Sikhs within India. But one result may be hundreds of millions of Islamic poor, and newly urbanized people who would have a special reason to then prefer the less dynamic, but in such a circumstance apparently more dependable authoritarian, economic organization of political Islam.

This mention of poverty may look odd in the context of the attacks of September 11th since the nineteen men who participated in those were mainly middle-class university graduates. But then, many of the leading lights in the old Communist parties were, for all the talk of the toiling masses, often middle-class university graduates, such as Marx, Lenin and Fidel Castro. It could turn out in both cases that it was great economic destitution that provided large numbers of people prepared to take orders from middle-class leaderships. In our post-September 11th situation, this would make for thousands of new recruits to terrorist groups. It's up to those trying to defeat terrorism to bring enough imagination and intelligence to bear on this situation to stop such a downward spiral. The economic arguments in these chapters are part of an attempt to contribute to this.

In this chapter, I examine what could happen in the next irregular growth phase of the long wave which, I argued in chapter 12, is due to start between 2015 and 2020. As a result of economic globalization, this would have worldwide effects. These effects make extremely grim reading.

Likely Effects of the Next Unreliable Growth Phase of the Long Wave

The Urbanized Countries

The greatest sufferers here would be the unemployed, of course, or people in employ with falling real incomes, but the urbanized countries would be able to support them on welfare payments, even though these would be austere. Black people in the United States and Britain, and other ethnic minorities in other countries who already do a disproportionate amount of the unskilled work, would suffer most. Thus, the gains in anti-racialism would be knocked back: black people would in all probability be disproportionately hit by such an economic development and their paths of advancement most blocked. Women who worked outside of the home could come under ferocious attack for taking jobs away from millions of unemployed men, suicide rates would shoot up and so on.

In such a situation in an urbanized country, various things can be done. The United States in the 1930s instituted the New Deal, but we should also be clear that Roosevelt's New Deal didn't solve American unemployment. Thus, according to Ross (*Causes and Consequences of the Great Depression,* Evans, London, 1994) unemployment was around thirteen million or about 25 percent of the work force when Roosevelt became President in 1933 and he reduced it by perhaps a third at best, to about eight million, in time for the 1936 election. This was the best achieved by the U.S. in the 1930s since in 1937 and 1938 unemployment climbed back to nine or ten million. Only the Japanese attack on Pearl Harbor at the end of 1941 ended American unemployment, which had stayed stubbornly high until then, which is where it had been since the crash of 1929, some twelve years earlier.

The "New Economy"

For much of the second half of the 1990s, there was much talk in the urbanized countries, and especially in the United States, that recessions were a thing of the past, thanks to a thing called the New Economy. This involved a continual improvement in productivity, which would continually lower prices, which would, therefore, keep consumption going up and up permanently, and so recessions would be a thing of the past, and the Dow Jones industrial average would hover around ten thousand pretty well permanently. Well, we both know it didn't happen, and we also know why. The reason is exceptionally familiar. The electronics sector of the economy was so profitable that many firms rushed into this area, but the rate of increase of sales was completely unsustainable and after a few years they had overproduction in this sector which couldn't be sold, and this had then to be scrapped at huge losses.

This recession proceeded even though the Federal Reserve bank lowered interest rates ten times during 2001, bringing them down to under two percent, a level previously seen in 1962. This still didn't stop the recession from developing.

This pattern of an inability to stop a recession from developing is similar to the experience during the twenty years from the early 1970s to the early 1990s. No measures adopted by the United States between the early 1970s and the early 1990s prevented a fall in real incomes of the bottom 20 percent of American earners to the level of the mid 1960s, or unemployment in the U.S. reaching 11 percent in 1982 and virtually no capitalist country elsewhere in the world was without similar problems.

There is also the fact that as more and more people live longer in the urbanized countries, we can expect to have a growing pool of people with ageing problems such as Alzheimer's disease and senile dementia, and no income, who would need to be cared for. This would be an absolute drain on scarce resources during a period of unreliable growth.

Overall, we would expect a growth of poverty in the urbanized countries after 2020.

The Urbanizing Countries

It is, of course, in the urbanizing countries that there are the greatest numbers of newly urban people. To get some small feel of how quickly this has all happened, and continues to happen, consider the following data from David Reynolds (*One World Divisible,* Penguin, Pg. 144).

Between 1950 and 1970, global population grew from about 2.5 billion to 3.6 billion. During that time the proportion living in urban areas grew from 28 percent to 38 percent, and in cities of over one hundred thousand from 16 percent to nearly 24 percent.

That increase from 28 to 38 percent of humanity that was living in urban conditions was a percentage increase of 10 percent, and it jumped by another 12 percent to a wholly unprecedented fifty percent of humanity living in urban connurbations of some kind by the end of the twentieth century. This was also 50 percent of six billion people, a figure passed in October 1999, as compared to 2.5 billion in 1950. (See also the very useful summary of our post September 11th environmental situation by Harvard Professor Edward O. Wilson, *Scientific American,* February 2002, pgs. 72–79.)

In the urbanizing countries, many people are first generation urban, and most are likely to lack the skills and capital to obtain good jobs, even if these were available. So, how, in conditions of unreliable economic growth lasting a couple of decades, would the hundreds of millions of unemployed newly urban people in urbanizing countries worldwide survive? Few of these states could afford welfare payments. No doubt, civil service jobs would be expanded, but these would not be remotely sufficient to cover more than a tiny fraction of the unemployed. Yet urban people, unlike their rural cousins, don't usually have the means to even grow their own food. There would be mass dependence on state or charitable handouts for something as basic as people's daily bread.

If people in the urbanizing countries can't buy fuel, there'll be an increase in their need to chop down trees for fire wood, and this will encourage soil erosion and the spread of deserts. As most of the urbanizing countries are importers of oil, they would be likely to have to cut their imports of oil. That might well increase deaths from the cold during winter.

Water Conflicts

There are still further likely problems. The world's population now tops six billion people, so that by the time the next long-term trough is due round between 2015–2020, the world's population is very likely to be above seven billion people. This growing world population will, amongst other things, require more and more fresh water. There have already been some threats of war over water resources, e.g. between Syria and Turkey, and between Egypt and Ethiopia, and in agreements signed by the Israelis and the Palestinians since the Oslo agreement of 1993, the Israelis have allocated 80 percent of the water in the area that they control to themselves. As all these countries live in, or close to, semi-desert conditions, so the potential political dynamite here is considerable. In our increasingly globalized world, the ability to insulate ourselves from the effects of such conflicts decreases all the time.

So, this unprecedented fraction of humanity that is now urban seems to me to have enormous consequences in the event of a long term phase of unreliable economic growth. Unemployment need not be all that high a fraction of all work-seekers, say 10 percent, for this to mean that the absolute number of people unemployed would be in the hundreds of millions. This seems to me to be extremely dangerous socially, and to be the sort of fact that would be likely to make numerous recruits for terrorism.

An increasingly globalized world makes this 50 percent of humanity that is urban increasingly part of a single world economy of some 3000 million consumers. Thus, in the years prior to 2015, globalization should produce very large markets for a vast range of goods and services, but that also means a great growth in productive capacity. This is not just a growth in the number of machines or their output but a continual growth in the average productivity of each worker. These considerations seem likely only added to by another. China, India, and Russia are three of the world's potentially biggest producers of finished industrial goods, but none have previously been major exporters of finished industrial products on the world stage. By the end of the year which saw the September 11th attacks, both China and Taiwan had joined the World Trade Organization, and by 2005, there seems little reason to think that China, India, and Russia will not all be full members of the WTO. These would constitute an enormous market, but if, as is likely, they too then become large exporters of industrial products, then a transition to an unreliable growth phase between 2015–2020 would leave vast new productive capacities underused, and with likely shrinking job opportunities, etc. This would likely further aggravate the depth of the fall in real incomes worldwide.

Accordingly, if, as a result of urbanization and globalization, we have a world of some three billion urban people, and the economy goes into a phase of unreliable growth, then the fall in living standards of the bottom 20 percent of the population could be dire. Also via the Internet, competition is tending to become thoroughly international and altogether more cut-throat and intense.

Of course, new commodities may appear during a downturn and do something to reduce falls in real incomes. But these may provide only small relief in a world economy of three billion urban consumers. For example, although personal computers were introduced on a considerable scale in 1981, when IBM began to manufacture them, the entire new computer industry probably did not provide more than a million new jobs throughout the entire world throughout the 1980s. This was at a time when registered unemployment worldwide in the urbanized countries alone was usually well above twenty million. The internet and mobile phone industries of the 1990s may not have provided much more than that either. So, there is absolutely no guarantee that the market will, at just the right time, itself produce new commodities whose production will be remotely sufficient to *prevent a serious fall in real incomes for a couple of decades.*

128

The Effect of Disease

As further hundreds of millions of people pour into the cities of the urbanizing countries, millions of inadequately fed people in close proximity to each other will make excellent carriers of every infectious disease available. The dish which is used in biology laboratories is called the Petrie dish, and to have millions of ill-fed people close together in urban slums and worldwide could be like having millions of people who would function like so many Petrie dishes in close proximity, and would thus considerably increase the chance of worldwide epidemics. One of America's notable science educators, Laurie Garrett, wrote a large book entitled *The Coming Plague* (Penguin 1995). This work lists the spread of such diseases as the Marburg Virus, Yellow Fever, Lassa Fever, Ebola, and of course, AIDS. Meanwhile, we still don't know what led the original plague to develop the way it did, and ravage the world for some three hundred and fifty years from about 1350 to 1700, which killed about a third of the people in the areas that it got to.

AIDS deserves a whole section to itself. By September 11th, twenty million had already died from AIDS and some thirty-six million were infected with HIV. Imagine a long phase of unreliable economic growth began between 2015–2020 and that no vaccine against AIDS had been discovered. By then, at least forty million would have died of AIDS and one shudders to think about the numbers infected. One hundred million? Two hundred million? Not merely would there be vast numbers of deaths from AIDS, but in a situation where the state already struggled just to feed millions of urban unemployed, there would likely be even less ability to pay for drugs which inhibit the development of AIDS amongst people who are already HIV-positive.

Such a development could easily fuel new hate stories. Thus, during the 1980s, the old Soviet Union tried alleging that AIDS had been invented by America as part of some nefarious but unexplained American plot against the people of the world. In the sort of situation now under consideration, where governments of urbanizing countries were struggling with both the appalling death rates from AIDS and also the challenge to be scientifically truthful about the way in which AIDS is usually transmitted—namely to wives and children by husbands and fathers, who in turn had infected themselves with prostitutes. In such a situation, the temptation to claim that AIDS was some sort of Jewish/Western/Capitalist/American plot would be enormous, especially if, like present-day South Africa, the size of the problem was so large that to spend money on even the cheapest drugs would be a severe drain on the health budget. This would be much more true in a long phase of unreliable economic growth.

We saw at the beginning of Part III that it was a previous trough of the fifty-year cycle that enabled the Nazis to attain state power. We saw there how in elections for the central parliament the percentage of the votes cast for the Nazis was 2.5 percent on May 20th 1928 but 18 percent on September 14th 1930, a peak of 42 percent on July 31st 1932. When we reflect on what could happen in the next long-term slowdown sketched in this chapter, the potential for some militant religious movement to be catapulted into state power in a large country, or perhaps in a number of smaller ones, seems high.

I conclude from all the other arguments above (that the sheer numbers now urbanized, and that many are first generation urban and that this is an unprecedentedly large fraction of a continually growing world population) that the effects of globalization will likely make the effects of the next period of unreliable economic growth after 2020 very serious.

So, for all these reasons, both economic and cultural, I conclude that groups like the ones that launched the attacks of September 11th would only massively grow in number and in degree of support. The attackers of September 11th came from an Islamic background and one feature here does seem to me worth observing. Islam is the dominant religious identity in some fifty countries, so the poverty and the dispersal into so many countries of the world's Muslims thereby lends itself for an unusually large fraction of Muslims to feel that there is some sort of dastardly attack by some worldwide force on Muslims, because they are Muslims.

To the extent that this is true seems to me to be one large reason why militants from an Islamic background may be especially prone to feel that they are being beaten because of their religious identity. Seldom do I see this feeling expressed, and because of the relative scarcity of expression I am going to have recourse to the most notorious Marxist who ever lived, namely the Marxist mass murderer, Joseph Stalin. In *Leninism,* Lawrence and Wishart, 1944, page 365, Stalin was quoted as having said in a speech in 1931:

> . . . We're a hundred years behind the advanced nations, and those who lag behind are beaten . . . One feature of the history of old Russia was the continual beatings she suffered for falling behind, for her backwardness. She was beaten by the Mongol Khans. She was beaten by the Turkish Beys. She was beaten by the Swedish feudal lords. She was beaten by the Polish and Lithuanian gentry. She was beaten by the British and French capitalists. She was beaten by the Japanese barons. All beat her for her backwardness: for military backwardness, for cultural backwardness, for political backwardness, for industrial backwardness, for agricultural backwardness. She was beaten because to do so was profitable and could be done with impunity.

This quote seems to me in many ways to sum up what I think the attackers of September 11th felt; they, too, felt that their worldwide religious community was being "beaten." Thus, a disproportionate fraction of "beatings" are indeed endured by Muslim communities. Perhaps the most notable was the destruction by Christian Europe of the Islamic Ottoman Empire, and it was this that led to the destruction in 1924 of the Islamic Caliphate. To get some very rough feel of what an equivalent in the Christian world *could* have felt like, let us imagine that the Italian Communist Party had taken power in Italy after the Second World War and deposed the Pope and destroyed the entire institution of the Papacy. Though the Caliphate was not a papacy, it had existed in some shape or form since the death of Mohammed in 632 CE, but overnight, it was just abolished by the newly secular Turkey.

Another source of being "beaten" has been military. Thus, in 1948, little Israel began its habit of repeatedly kicking in the teeth of mainly Muslim Arab fighters from within mainly Muslim Arab peoples who outnumbered Israel's population by thirty or forty to one and which refused to recognize Israel's right to exist. Since 1948, too, India has thrashed Islamic Pakistan and stamped on the Islamic people of Kashmir. Then, the Bosnian Serbs in the 1990s carried out the slaughter of perhaps a hundred thousand Bosnian Muslims, and finally the entry in 1991 of Christian American troops into Saudi Arabia which contains Islamic shrines at Mecca and Medina.

I would summarize these "beatings" of Muslims as follows:

1. Presence of Christian American troops (infidels!) in the Islamic holy land that contains Mecca and Medina.
2. American bombardment of Muslims in Iraq 1990 to the present day.
3. Attacks on Muslim communities 1945 have included Bosnia, Chechnya, Cyprus, Kashmir, Nigeria, and the West Bank and Gaza Strip.
4. Israeli humiliation of Muslim (and Christian) Arabs and general Israeli tendency to show feelings of swaggering superiority, and all this on ground on which, until 1948, scores of mosques stood.
5. To the extent that there is a religion of the world's poor, that religion is arguably Islam, so ostentatious American wealth and luxury can easily seem yet a further insult.
6. Individualist fragmentation of the whole collectivist

132

communal ethic of Islam, which superficial people find easy to blame on its most open aggressive exponent, namely America.

From all this it seems to me that Muslims who do feel strongly that they are part of one big Muslim community, or umma, could easily feel that to be a Muslim in today's world is to experience oneself as being "beaten," and more than anything else being thus beaten by big strong America.

If what I have said of the objective strengths of liberal capitalism is broadly right, then the fact that most Muslims do not live in conditions of liberal capitalism and are so spread out amongst perhaps a quarter of the countries of the world, does leave them weak and vulnerable. Meanwhile, it seems that no other system than liberal capitalism does more to guarantee the long-term survival of humanity. All this puts Islamic militancy in a hopeless conflict that it is exceptionally unlikely to win, but by which they are bound to feel very "beaten."

We may see this conclusion in another way. Islam as a particular kind of authoritarian community is indeed under attack, not altogether unlike the way the communal nature of Roman Catholicism is increasingly fragmenting. This process also became extremely visible within the Republic of Ireland in the 1980s. Prior to this, the Irish as a people seem to have often taken immense pride in the number of priests and religious people they produced. Now, this is in obvious decline. This is especially interesting since Ireland has had a long terrorist tradition, too, namely that involving the Irish Republican Army. The socio-economic changes wrought by ideological domination by an urban capitalist way of life in Ireland have increasingly rendered the IRA irrelevant; a similar change in other traditional religious communities around the world would be especially attractive, but it is very difficult to achieve in the short term.

If to all this we add the conclusions of the long waves, we see that there is an economically generated potential for grim conflict.

My conclusion from the considerations that I have produced in this chapter is that some new measures that might reduce the extent of, or even abolish, a serious long term loss in the standard of living of the bottom 20 percent of the population, must be taken *before* the end of the second decade of our new century. In short, they must be extra measures at least begun during the phase of reliable economic growth. That, I will argue, is what is now possible for the first time; I am going to argue that it is possible to take measures during the first half of the fifty-year cycle to *prevent or greatly mitigate* long-term falls in the real income. What I think these measures are will be the subject of my next chapter.

IV
Bringing the Pieces Together

14

First Step to Fight Terrorism:
A Use of Economic Boom

We saw in Chapter 13 how the effects of a prolonged slowdown, which is due to begin in the second half of the second decade of our new century, could be especially grim, given the newly urbanized state of so many hundreds of millions of people. In Chapter 12, I argued that the probability of serious long-term fall in real incomes of the bottom 20 percent was very great, unless successful steps were taken to prevent this. To see what step we need to take to prevent such a negative effect of the next economic restructuring phase, we must consider some facts about powering by fossil fuels.

Power from Fossil Fuels and Further Industrialization

To generate electricity from fossil fuels such as coal or oil has large problems for many urbanizing countries:

1. To increase production in the urbanizing countries would mean pouring greatly increased amounts of carbon dioxide into the atmosphere of the world. Thus, to bring all the people of the world up to a standard of living enjoyed by the average person in the United States might, with our current use of fossil fuels to generate

power, produce so much more carbon dioxide in the atmosphere as to cause all the ice in Antarctica to melt. This last is a very extreme scenario: were this to occur, the estimates are that this could cause a rise in the sea level of seventy-five meters, or two hundred and forty feet. However, it is not wholly absurd and indeed, as this is being written, an internationally funded eight-year project is underway to drill into Antarctica to discover its history during previous periods of raised temperatures on earth. The obvious fear from such an extreme change is that many of the world's capital cities which are currently at sea-level would then stand in danger of being completely flooded out by such a rise in sea level. The cultural loss, and indeed productive loss, for all of humanity from this would be utterly vast. Such a rise in the sea can't be allowed to happen, if it is at all avoidable.

2. The replacement of human energy with non-human energy was a crucial part of raising the standard of living. One does not need to go into statistic after statistic from the Industrial Revolution about steam engines, windmills, and the like to see the truth of this. But, in urbanizing countries, the road system is far too primitive to transport fossil fuels like oil and coal into large parts of the rural areas where considerable minorities, at least, of their people still live. Oil pipelines can be laid, but this only makes any economic sense when the consumers are not too spread out from each other. But that is exactly what rural people tend to be, almost by definition. Accordingly, its very difficult and very expensive to transport large amounts of fossil fuels such as oil very far inland. Just look on a map at the huge distances that exist in some of the newly urbanizing countries—e.g. India, China, the Republic of the Congo, Brazil, etc.

These are simply huge countries and the difficulty and expense of transporting fossil fuels around the country is evidently a large added cost to any economic activity. Once some fossil fuel has been burnt, it has been destroyed and more fuel is needed to replace it. This requires more of it, more expense in transportation, etc.

3. The ability to transport fossil fuels into the interior of a large country assumes that roads once built have been adequately maintained, but this is also extremely difficult, and the lack of a reliable source of funding year after year to do this has had disastrous effects on infrastructure in many of these countries.

4. Many urbanizing countries are importers of oil, and some of coal. How much they can import depends on reserves of foreign currency—something which all countries which are both non-oil producing and urbanizing countries are especially likely to lack!

5. The problem mentioned above in 4. is only added to by the habit of oil producers like OPEC to push up the price of their oil during rapid periods of economic growth. This practice is an enormous attack on the foreign reserves of most urbanizing countries; to get rid of such behavior would greatly help the urbanizing countries to close the gap with the urbanized countries.

These five considerations are all large fetters on economic growth of large minorities at least of the world's population, who live in the rural areas of the urbanizing countries.

From all these considerations a crucial part of the way to prevent or largely alleviate the negative effects of the next economic downturn should be clear: that is to use the increased public income from the boom part of the economic cycle to finance research and development into non-polluting sources of energy to produce electricity at prices equal to or cheaper than its production by coal or other fossil fuels would. I say that, provided this were available *on time, i.e. by the time the next slowdown is due, that could have the requisite economic impact to prevent or largely reduce the negative effects on real incomes which is threatened by the next cyclical slowdown. Thus, if the cheap electricity came, for instance, from solar panels, it would have the immense advantage in the rural areas of the urbanizing countries, many of which are tropical countries: since solar panels have no moving parts, they should require no routine maintenance whatsoever. Most of the least economically developed countries have the space available on which to have large banks of cells, and a good deal of sun to help their electrical output. In the urbanized countries, and in, perhaps, the urban parts of the urbanizing countries, too, wind power must be one strong candidate to produce cheap power. Once electricity can be generated cheaply, hydrogen cells which produce only water could also be cheaply produced to power vehicles of all kinds, and not burn oil to power these. This could revolutionize agriculture of the urbanizing countries since in this way agricultural vehicles of all kinds could be thereby powered and enable humanity to feed the expected ten billion people by mid century without nearly as much destruction of forests that current technology would imply. (On the environmental aspects, see Edward O. Wilson, Scientific American,* February 2002, pgs. 72–79.)

Although spending by private companies, including some of the world's biggest oil companies such as BP, would eventually bring down the costs of providing electricity in non-polluting ways, there is no guarantee that they would finance this in time to prevent or greatly alleviate the negative effects of the next slowdown. That is why public funding through the tax system is needed, and is best done before we reach the slowdown phase of the long wave. We can see an example of this in the writings of an extreme optimist in environmental matters, Bjorn Lomborg, who estimates that price of generating energy by renewable means will only fall below the price of doing this by fossil fuels in 2030. (See *The*

Skeptical Environmentalist, Cambridge University Press 2001, p. 119, et seq.) The oil exporters already keep the price of oil relatively low much of the time to discourage large amounts of research in non-polluting energy sources. Thus, once oil prices slumped in the 1980s, the resources going into research and development of these sources of energy declined, after a brief period of enthusiasm, when the price of oil quadrupled in 1973. It would, on the arguments of this book, *play into the hands of the terrorists to wait until 2030 for cheap electricity to be available to be produced by renewable means to replace the burning of fossil fuels.*

It could be argued that the oil producers like OPEC could price the new non-polluting sources of energy out of the market if they were to sufficiently reduce the price that they charged for their oil. To this objection there are several answers. Firstly, the United States is a large importer of oil, so for the United States to spend on research to bring down the costs of non-polluting sources of energy would save the United States massively on the cost of current oil imports that would continue until these other sources of energy replaced the burning of oil. In addition, as the price of oil fell, some oil fields that are currently economic to tap would cease to be so, unless prices of extraction also fell enough to compensate. So, falling sale prices would actually help to create a shortage of available oil, odd as this must seem at first sight. In addition to this, the transportation of fossil fuel is sufficiently labor intensive and difficult for there to be minimum prices below which fossil fuel prices just could not go. These would continue to apply to inland parts of the urbanizing countries because of the difficulties, which I discussed earlier, of transporting fossil fuels to these areas. So, an approach which tried to price lower-cost renewables out of the market by lowering the cost of fossil fuels by their producers would thus encounter some definite failures. Of course, if the price of oil came down, there would be a period in which more people would burn more petrol in their cars, and, so, make pollution worse. In that case, the aim of replacing oil with renewable sources of energy would be strengthened by the effects of that increased pollution.

Certainly, great strides have already been made in bringing down the costs of electricity generated by wind power as compared to electricity generated by burning coal. Thus, as previously noted in chapter 11, during the last twenty-five years of the twentieth century, the cost to generate a kilowatt of electricity by means of wind-power cost dropped to about one-twelfth of what it had cost twenty-five years earlier. This improvement arose because the decline had been from fifty American cents to generate a kilowatt of power using wind-power to four American cents. That was a good advance, but on the day of the attacks on New York and Washington, it still only cost two American cents to generate the same amount of energy using coal. There was, thus, still some way to go. There are also other problems that must be overcome, such as a loss of economies of scale, because wind-power generators are inevitably smaller than those powered by fossil fuels. A larger number of wind-power generators is needed to generate the same amount of power, and this raises cost.

To definitively demonstrate that the achievement of cheap non-polluting energy available anywhere on Earth would be sufficient to prevent a large fall in long-term real incomes during the next long-term slowdown might seem very difficult or even impossible. For, it would depend on industrialization then being able to be pursued by the urbanizing countries, and for this to occur a good many factors would all have to come together in the same place. There would need to be enough capital, the appropriate skills would need to be available, there would need to be political stability, adequate savings or an ability to borrow at interest rates that were not punitively high, and so on. There is one very good piece of news that is often overlooked in discussions of underdevelopment. This is that just two countries between them contain fully one-third of all of the world's people, both have so far demonstrated adequate political stability, one has recently been admitted to the World Trade Organization, both have pretty good recent histories of sensible economic policies, and so on. The two countries I have in mind are, of course, India and China. If just these two countries were able to make use of cheap, non-polluting power available at any place in their own countries, to develop their countries and thereby greatly increase what they traded with the rest of the world, and especially if the main momentum for this got going between 2015–2020 when the next slowdown is due, then the prospects for reducing a fall in real living standards thanks to that next slowdown of the long wave seem to me to be reasonably bright.

Obviously, a great mass of details would need to be thought through, but that seems to me just one of the tasks to be performed in the years prior to when the next slowdown is to be expected. I should add that there is already some such being discovered by the education and science arm of the United Nations, UNESCO, which has a ten-year program of installing solar-powered plants in rural areas to power distance learning in many urbanizing countries, for the substantial fraction of the population still in the countryside. Some of the work being done in the program has been written up in *The Timeless Energy of the Sun,* ed. Madanjeet Singh, Thames and Hudson, 1998. Right now, perhaps only a third of people in the world have a regular supply of electric power at all, let alone have a source that they could productively use as people in the urbanized countries daily use it. Although one needs a whole collection of things for a growth in the standard of living, cheap reliable solar power would be a massive step forward for perhaps forty percent of the world's people, or some two and a half billion people. That is an enormous potential market, which is one reason that I predict it is the biggest single step needed to prevent the next long-term economic slowdown which otherwise we could expect to start between 2015–2020. Obviously, the United States and the European Union need to greatly reduce subsidies to their farmers, so as to import food from the urbanizing countries.

So, my first proposal is that, once the recession of the first couple of years of our new twenty-first century is over, during what remains of the fairly full employment phase of our present cycle, when public money is at its easiest to obtain, we consciously press forward with research and development money into producing electricity cheaply from photo-voltaic cells and wind-power, in the sort of time frame I have been talking about. Certainly, there are precedents for this. On July 29th 1958 the United States responded to the launching of Sputnik 1 nine months earlier by setting up the tax-payer funded National Aeronautics and Space Administration, NASA, to catch up with the Soviets. This, the Americans managed within eleven years when Neil Armstrong and Buzz Aldrin landed on the moon, on July 20th 1969. My proposal is that something comparable to this, or to the National Cancer Institute within National Institutes of Health, be formed for the non-polluting energy field. Thus, within the Department of Energy, this could be something like a Renewable Energy Acceleration Committee or REAC. This is my first proposal to tackle the next long-term period of hesitant growth, with all its implications for the growth of terrorism.

It is worth noting that during the non-expansionist phases that have been so far, there has been extensive restructuring with less profitable industries either closing down altogether or moving elsewhere. These processes would still go on, but the new commodity area or areas should be able to reduce unemployment from those declining areas of economic activity. Hopefully, the transition to a more service-based economy means that there is less variety in occupations between industries, and so it will be easier for workers to move from a declining industry to an expanding one.

It would be a very large boon if the urbanized countries installed enough of the same ways of generating this cheap electricity to pay the development costs of these sources of energy. Obviously, the urbanizing countries are in no position to pay these development costs. This pattern, whereby it is we in the urbanized world who pay the development costs, is already the pattern with numerous drugs, such as those which slow down the development of AIDS. It's only because the people of the urbanized countries have paid these development costs, that the drugs companies can make large cuts to what they charge the urbanizing countries for these identical drugs.

For urbanized countries, like America, who use so much electricity, solar cells would probably play a subsidiary role to some other non-polluting source of electricity such as wind power. We therefore need to do enough publicly-financed investment to bring down the costs of things like wind power. The achievement of this would bring another great boon, namely the ability to charge up fuel cells from such power, and this would mean that humanity could cease to burn oil in cars, lorries, trucks and agricultural vehicles of all kinds. This would greatly improve food production, although to make best use of this worldwide would mean that the urbanized countries would have to be prepared to import a good deal more of their food from outside countries. This, of course, means difficulties with domestic farming communities, and it also has military implications, since no country can be safe during a war if too much of its food is imported.

Oil-Exporting Countries

If most of the oil used in the world is not used for powering things such as vehicles of all kinds or to generate electricity, then this has large implications for the economies of the oil-exporting countries. However, the overall effects might not be anything like as negative as might at first sight appear. Hundreds of products of high value are actually made from oil, such as plastics, paints and industrial chemicals, whilst fertilizer is often made from the natural gas found with oil. A world economy one and a half times, say, the size of the one which existed on September 11th would need about one and a half times more of all of these. In such increased demand is the chance for the oil exporting countries to export oil in the form of these finished products, rather than as raw oil. This could broadly maintain the revenues that these countries enjoy from their oil, even if the volumes exported were substantially smaller. This fact is an example of a point I made in chapter 11, namely that countries with prosperous populations are ones which export finished goods which contain the skilled labor of their own nationals. Indeed, only in one or two unusual countries, like Kuwait, where a tiny population sits on huge oil reserves, is there any prosperity without that country including amongst its exports a considerable volume of finished goods. Certainly, to depend only on the export of raw materials is to almost ensure a country in which poverty is endemic, and for whom respect is low.

Withdrawal of Troops from Saudi Arabia

In conditions in which humanity doesn't power economic activity from oil, by burning it, any oil imports would have a greatly reduced strategic importance. In that situation, the United States could withdraw the troops from Saudi Arabia, which it has had there since 1990 when Saudi Arabia was first threatened by Iraq. The presence of these troops causes disquiet amongst Muslims generally and outrage amongst Islamic militants. The latter, especially, seem to see the presence of Christian troops in Saudi Arabia with its two Islamic holy places of Mecca and Medina as a case of religious rape. The Christian Crusaders have gotten hold of an innocent Muslim girl and they have violated her, they are continuing to violate her, and they show no signs of contrition or apology, and certainly not to Allah. Indeed, it is quite possible that on the very land where Mohammed and his wives and companions once walked and discussed and prayed together, Christian American troops now drink beer and other alcoholic drinks, and as the U.S.

army now contains troops of both sexes, fornicate as well. Whilst the major economies of the world are powered by burning large amounts of oil, those troops will stay, and Islamic militants will dream of terrorist attacks on us. As I have noted above, even if many attempts can be thwarted by vigilance by the security authorities, some are pretty well certain to succeed. The success of the writers of computer viruses in outwitting the firewall software and anti-virus software on computers may be a grimly accurate model of this uncomfortable truth.

Even if the development of renewable energy were accelerated and had the effect I have suggested it would have on preventing the negative income effects of what otherwise would have been the next non-expansionary period, there remains the facts about the evolution and spread of new diseases. The prevention in growth in economic poverty would retard the problems here, but they would not stop them. So we need a further project to tackle this.

Second Proposal

Although there have been large advances in understanding, I am struck by how slow has been the advance in medical combating of diseases like AIDS and cancer. As noted in chapter 11, as long ago as 1971, President Richard Nixon got Congress to set up a separate cancer research unit within the National Institute of Health, and by the 1990s, this unit was getting some two billion dollars each and every year for research. Yet, all the massive efforts these past fifty years around the world have only added something like five years to the life of the average cancer patient. The rate at which HIV evolves to full-blown AIDS can be slowed, but so far, that seems to be it.

It might be thought that most of the cancer deaths are in the rich, highly urbanized countries, but unfortunately, the cigarette companies are now targeting people in the urbanizing world, as the companies have been so battered in the urbanized world. It's a dreadful fact, but the numbers of cancer deaths in the urbanizing world may well overtake the urbanized world by the middle of the twenty-first century. So, this very slow growth in the life expectancy of a cancer patient will affect far more people around the world.

Now, I think I know at least one reason why there's been only slow growth in improving life expectancy of cancer patients. It's similar to why progress against AIDS, though fast by the standards of the past, is appallingly slow relative to present need. To see what I'm getting at look at the world's cadre of scientists; they are drawn predominantly from the one billion people who live in North America and Europe. *That is, most of the world's scientists are drawn from about one-sixth of the world's people.* Now as a non-racialist, I assume that this ultimately European origin of most of the world's scientists has nothing whatsoever to do with human biology, nothing whatsoever to do with any biological or genetic constraint within non-European human beings. *In that case, we're still wasting some five-sixths of the world's potential scientists.* In this first half of the twenty-first century, it's biology and bio-chemistry which are the sciences which are poised for the greatest advances. As we saw in the chapter which dealt with what could go wrong in a long-term slowdown, AIDS continues to ravage sub-Saharan Africa. Only six weeks after the attacks on the World Trade Center, the South African Institute of Medical Research predicted that, by 2010, 40 percent of deaths of adults in South Africa will be from AIDS and that this will mean some five to seven million such deaths. How many millions of children this will leave orphaned at an early age can only be guessed at, but being orphaned before the age of about twenty usually does end up doing psychological damage. The work of the attachment theorists in psychology is important here. Meanwhile, HIV is spreading to Eastern Europe and the Caribbean, and also infecting large populations in China, Indonesia and other huge populations in Asia. That is what we're up against at this time, without adding any of the other diseases already identified as leading to another worldwide plague. So, my second proposal should be fairly clear, and that is to use our current fairly full employment conditions to at least double our worldwide cadre of biologists and biochemists from people in the newly urbanizing countries, and to at least double our world scientific research labor force in disease areas like AIDS, cancer and tropical diseases. It is only by means of improved prevention, and quicker more effective interventions when disease does hit, that we can contain the soaring costs of ill health, which threaten to suck up such large fractions of our surplus that other improvements, such as those in education, will fail to occur. By situating laboratories in the urbanizing countries, themselves, success can be enhanced. Thus, after Vietnam allowed more contact between its people and foreigners in the late 1980s, the Welcome Institute in London, a group which finances research in biology and biochemistry, set up a laboratory in Vietnam, and ten years later, they had made considerable improvements in the treatment of malaria. One reason was that the researchers in Vietnam had direct experience of malaria, something researchers in North America and Europe would be unlikely to have. (*Source:* BBC World Service broadcast, Friday, 14th December 2001.) Here is one example that needs to be multiplied thousands of times.

The adoption of these two proposals seem to me to be able to prevent or very largely alleviate the negative effects of the next long-term slowdown. With these stated, I would now like to add to my argument by turning to a historical question posed by these two proposals.

149

The Great Growth in Productivity in the Last Quarter of the Twentieth Century

If it is going to be possible to prevent the next economic downturn by actually developing cheap electricity from non-polluting sources like the sun, then the question arises as to why this sort of solution hasn't been done before. Why hasn't there been the spending of money during a boom to develop new commodities which would create new employment during the down phase? Was it possible, but the idea hadn't been proposed? I am going to argue that it was not possible to prevent serious unemployment in the way that I propose it could now be done, which is, ultimately, through the free market.

The Past Impossibility of This Kind of Solution

It is the major contention of my discussion of economics that the growth of scientific and technological advance during the last quarter of the twentieth century was so great that it now makes possible the sort of solution to long-term economic slowdown that I am proposing. This would also suggest that this solution would have been impossible in the past and that is what I shall now argue. I will illustrate what I think is at stake here with an example.

The date of September 11th, 2001 will be remembered for a long time, especially by Americans, but I noted at the beginning of this book that this date was not wholly different in its effect on Americans and others in the West from that of October 4th, 1957, when the then Soviet Union launched its first satellite, Sputnik 1, into orbit around the Earth.

Now, I wish to give a further reason for us to keep these two dates together. Both occurred at comparable places in the long-run economic cycle which lasts about fifty years; in each case, the date was about ten years into its predominantly good growth phase, and there was perhaps fifteen years to go before the onset of the next phase of hesitant growth. Now, let us imagine that President Eisenhower's Scientific Advisory Committee, then in the charge of James R. Killian, had tried in October, 1957, to think up ways in which scientific research could reduce future unemployment, the development of which in America reduces America's leadership position in the world. Let us further imagine that they came to ask themselves this question because some members of this committee had studied economic history and had noticed that things by and large got more difficult after 1873 for about twenty years, and that there had also been large panics in the U.S. in 1873 and 1893, and an agricultural depression in the U.S. in the 1870s and 1880s. Let us imagine that they had also had at their disposal the sort of table of economic development that I produced previously, and they could see that as these things go in cycles of about fifty years, they had correctly guessed in 1957 that 1973, not unlike 1873, would also be an important watershed year. In that case, what is the chance that this committee *could* in 1957 have looked around for some developing area of the economy whose development they could have accelerated by tax-payers' dollars so as to reduce unemployment during the next unreliable growth phase? Notice that the question I ask is not about the development of new products for the military—for which America for one has been spending lavishly since 1940—but tax-payer funded research during the predominant growth phase to accelerate the discovery of new *commodities* for the mass market whose production and sale would occur so as to provide serious amounts of new employment during the next period of hesitant growth.

Firstly, we must ask what industry or industries the committee would have chosen to accelerate with tax-payers' dollars, and there seems little doubt that in 1957, the committee would have chosen the industry which had been demonstrating for over ten years that it had the greatest potential for development, namely electronics, centered on the transistor. This already attracted much military funding for military purposes, something which increased after the Sputnik scare, but as I have already remarked the question I am asking relates not to producing items of super-high reliability that the military need and expect, and where expense is no object, but to producing items for the mass market for unemployment prevention. What actually occurred in the development of electronics centered on the transistor was:

1. The first transistor was made to work in the dying days of 1947.
2. The internet was first seriously worked on by America's Department of Defense's Defense Advanced Research Projects Agency, DARPA, from 1969 onwards.
3. The first integrated chip, the Intel 4004, was produced in 1971.
4. The first IBM PC was produced in 1981.
5. The mobile phone got going as a mass popular item in about 1991.
6. The internet only got going as a mass item once it was possible to call up the internet browser with a single mouse click via Microsoft's Windows 95 interface, which Microsoft rolled out in August 1995.

Only after the last time in each case did the new area give rise to commodities which provided some new employment. But would it have made scientific and industrial sense, given the capabilities that existed in 1957, that the government pour money into research and developments in electronics to as to speed up developments by say ten years so as to reduce unemployment in the next potential downturn? This would have required that the internet have been first proposed in 1959, that the first microchip be produced by the mid-1960s, that there had existed some version of Microsoft by the mid-late 1960s so as to be able to produce both the hardware and the software of the personal computer by say

1971. The mobile phone would have needed to have been in use by millions of people by 1981 and the internet would have to have been in use as a mass consumer item by 1985.

For, had such acceleration occurred, the personal computer would have provided some extra new employment in the difficult decade of the 1970s and the mobile phone and the internet would have provided some further new employment in the economically difficult decade of the 1980s. For one thing, these developments would have given hundreds of thousands and perhaps even a million or so young people around the world a new area to study, which would have kept them from the employment market for a few years and this would also have required the employment of scores of thousands of new teachers worldwide, and provided quite a number of jobs for less-skilled people.

It seems to me fairly clear that it would have been very unlikely that the developments which actually occurred *could* have been speeded up by about ten years to provide such beneficial effects on unemployment. I'm old enough to remember the state of electronic technology in 1960, when I was just starting out in this field, and when I asked questions about transistors, the old radio tube was still so popular then that I was advised to "stick to tubes." True, IBM had built all-transistor computers by then, like the IBM 1620. But in 1960, IBM's system 360 was still four years away, and then it had cost several billion dollars to develop. I have already mentioned various other successes that would have been needed to accelerate the developments that did occur by just ten years and looking back at the state technology was in I find it *very difficult to believe that this could have been done.*

Then there is the problem that such reductions in the fall of real incomes via accelerating the development of electronics, even if it had been successfully done, would at best have been mainly in the urbanized countries. Although the woes of the African continent became a subject much discussed in the 1970s and 1980s, the discussions of these almost always abstracted from the operation of the long waves of the world capitalist economy, whereas these difficulties were in considerable part, and perhaps even mainly, a consequence of the fact that the capitalist world economy was in its hesitant growth phase.

It should be obvious that *if* what I am now proposing was impossible during the previous period of good growth, i.e. accelerating a couple of crucial areas during the period 1948 to 1973 to help reduce falls in real incomes between 1973 to 1995, then this was even more impossible at still earlier cycles. Thus, there seems no chance that with the science of, say, 1907, a suitable research project initiated then could have accelerated the production of new commodities to be available in the 1920s and 1930s, to have reduced unemployment of those two decades, lessened the chances of the Nazis attaining office, or any other such desirable aim.

Contrast the situation in 1957 with the situation that we were in on the day of the attacks in New York and Washington; we can now propose a project of considerable complexity, namely getting the cost of electricity from renewable sources down below what fossil fuels could manage, even with improvements in their production of energy. Again, the sheer growth of knowledge and productivity of scientists during the last thirty years of the twentieth century becomes apparent. This is why we can now plan the prevention of the negative effects of a potential long-term economic downturn.

Nuclear Power

I have advocated that State finance be used to fund research and development of renewable energy and, in our post September 11th situation, military considerations must lead to increased questions of nuclear power. This is the obvious use of nuclear power stations as targets onto which to smash hijacked aircraft at top speed for maximum effect. Although various security measures are now being put into place to make this more difficult, none of these is 100 percent foolproof. I have already discussed in chapter 1 how it seems to me a virtual certainty that amongst all the thousands of regular airline pilots around the world, there will be a few who are political militants of one kind or another. The chances of at least one of these crashing a plane onto some chosen target within ten years of the attacks of September 11th must be very very high. In this regard it's worth noting that some thirteen weeks after the attacks of September 11th, on December 13th 2001, five armed men attacked India's parliament building, and twelve people died. Somebody is very likely to eventually use an aircraft to carry out such an operation. In our post-September 11th world, it would be best if there were no nuclear power stations lying helplessly on the ground, waiting to be hit, since the effects of success could be especially disastrous. These could include having to evacuate a huge population, perhaps from some major world city, which was downwind from such a power station.

A Replacement for the Proposals of Keynes

Until now, there has been Keynes' argument that a government could get itself out of a fall in income in a downturn by increasing aggregate demand. But one large problem with this is the sheer vastness of the money required to do this, and this at a time of small or even negative economic growth. To assume that this could be done to an adequate extent came perhaps more easily in the 1930s to an economist writing in London in what was still the center of the world's largest empire than it would to an economist of the present-day in say India or Brazil. One of Keynes' remedies for this was for the state to borrow, but this has led to the growth of the national debt on which interest payments must then be made. In the meantime, the New Deal, which was somewhat Keynesian in its financing, did not abolish unemployment, it only reduced it by a maximum of a third for a couple of years, namely 1935 and 1936, from the peak level of unemployment in early 1933. The New Deal just wasn't big enough, for one thing. Also, once the economic cycle has reached its usual low growth stage, it's very difficult to then start to think of commodities to produce that don't compete with already existing production. That is one reason why the New Deal concentrated on forms of infrastructure, like the Tennessee Valley Authority, the construction of about a million kilometers of roads within the United States, buildings for various city administrations and the like.

In addition to the Keynesians, we have had the so-called supply-side people, who stress that during a downturn, one should push down costs of production, and abolish various restraints on trade. My proposal is a mixture of these two: it would increase demand, but it is also a supply-side solution because it does involve the supply of something new, which results from the accelerated introduction of one or more new commodities to be bought and sold in the usual market way.

Kyoto

This raises the question of whether President Bush, in 2001, was right not to support the Kyoto agreement which aimed to cut carbon emissions to 5 percent below what they had been in 1990. There was nothing magical about the emissions of 1990 that made these the obvious measures to use, but they seem to have been chosen purely for convenience. The question to my mind is not whether we can sit back and do nothing, which I certainly think not. But perhaps for once Bjorn Lomborg (*The Skeptical Environmentalist,* Cambridge University Press, 2001, p. 303) is right in calculating that the costs of implementing Kyoto could be $346 billion a year, by the United States, Europe, Japan, Canada, Australia, and New Zealand. Compared to this, the cost of doing enough research and development to bring down the price of generating electricity by means of renewables starts to sound cheap. According to Margolis and Kammen, Energy Policy 27(10): 575–84 (quoted by Lomborg p. 287) the spending in the United States on renewable energy was just $200 million a year by the late 1990s. I have already noted that the United States government, through its National Cancer Institute within the National Institutes of Health, was spending some two billion dollars annually in each year of the 1990s. So, if there were a good reason to do so, there is already a good precedent to spend ten times that $200 million a year, which is what two billion dollars a year would be, on research and development of renewable energy. From these figures alone, we can see that to spend two billion dollars a year for fifteen years would come to something like thirty-five billion dollars, allowing for some inflation over the period. Also it seems as though two billion dollars a year for some fifteen years spent on research and development of renewables would be enough to bring the cost of generating electricity from them down to a competitive 0.8c/kwh by around 2015. So, provided at an early date the United States government put an adequate amount of money into research to seriously accelerate the downward movement of the costs of renewable energy, the United States government would be able to deflect much or even all of the criticism of its withdrawal from the Kyoto agreement.

The Largeness of the Boom between 1948 and 1973

Although the long wave theory would have predicted a period of expansion from the late 1940s until the early 1970s, it could not predict the size of that expansion, which in this period was simply unprecedented. It seems to me that the sheer size of this boom was much helped by the large wartime developments in research. The U.S., Britain, and Germany between them

157

newly-produced nuclear power, the jet aircraft, intercontinental rockets, penicillin, and the electronic computer. The United States is also said by David Reynolds (*One World Divisible,* Penguin, 2000, p. 495) to have spent some three billion dollars during the war developing radar and technical developments in this field, and is likely to have helped expand another considerable source of new employment after 1945, namely the television industry. The great advances in rockets later developed into a whole new industry of communication satellites. Another offshoot were spy satellites, which also provided some fresh employment and were arguably also a great step forward in globalization, for they made it much more difficult for one country to prepare a surprise attack on another country All these were new or expanded industries that led to large new commodity items from the late 1940s onwards, and the increased economic activity that they produced helped to produce the unprecedented boom that characterized the years between about 1948 and 1973. The development of those new commodities and some of their derivatives still feed our economy to this day. Arguably, the capitalist economies started to slow down their growth by the early 1970s partly because these new industries had been developed as far as they could go at the time, the numbers of people employed in them was by then shrinking as efficiency and productivity of producing those items themselves improved, and the new economic activities that they had enabled had by then ceased to grow fast, or even at all. To avoid long-term falls in real incomes in the future means continually looking for areas of science and technology to accelerate with public funds to provide new commodities which will provide fresh employment in the ordinary market way.

One final thought. The fact that periods of predominant economic growth have alternated with periods of predominant non-expansion might lead one to think that this was simply unchangeable. In this regard, notice that slavery once seemed every bit as universal and inevitable. Indeed, so unquestioned in principle was slavery as to be accepted in both the holy books of the Jews and the Muslims, and Jesus' disciple Paul advised a slave who had absconded to return to his master. So, slavery seems alive and well in the allegedly holy thinking of all three of our monotheisms, Judaism, Christianity and Islam. As I say, that is how widespread slavery was. But since about 1800, slavery has receded, and is now no longer explicitly practiced anywhere in the world. That isn't because we suddenly became nicer people, but because humanity produced its way out of slavery. So something that had gone on for thousands of years finally came to an end when Saudi Arabia finally outlawed slavery in 1962, and Oman followed suit in 1970. I say that it's the same with long periods of unreliable growth—we now have the wherewithal to produce our way out of cycles of long-term economic slowdown, which is the only way in which it could be done.

15

Second Step to Contain Terrorism:
Terrorism, Democracy and Law

I have no expertise in international law, and this chapter is offered mainly as a provocation to try to stimulate some thought, by applying the themes of this book.

One major theme has been the centrality of democracy, and democracy can only work, it seems to me, if the state alone has legitimacy of violence. Terrorism, apart from being violence directed at private individuals, to me represents a *privatization* of maiming and killing, and it seems to me that this is a profoundly anti-democratic development. The fact that the Americans sometimes charge states like Iraq and Iran with "state-sponsored terrorism" only adds to the implication that states themselves can't be guilty of terrorism, only groups of private individuals can be, but terrorism *can* be sponsored by a state if they receive ongoing support from that state.

Then there is the character of the crimes with which a state may be charged, as distinct from the crimes with which a group of individuals may be charged. A state may be charged with war crimes, or crimes against humanity for instance, as Mr. Milosevic in his capacity as President of Serbia has been for the events in the Balkans in the 1990s. He has not, however, been charged with terrorism, although he plainly used terror. Nor is the dictator of Iraq charged with terrorism in respect of his gassing of the Kurds in 1988; again he has faced allegations of genocide or crimes against humanity. By contrast, the single man who it is thought was due to join the nineteen attackers who died on September 11th, but had been detained by the American authorities a couple of weeks before the attacks of September 11th, has not been charged with war crimes or genocide or crimes against humanity.

There is another reason for my belief that the term terrorism should be restricted to groups of private individuals, and this is a practical reason. In the days immediately after September 11th, the American government demanded of the regime in Afghanistan that they hand over Osama Bin Laden, and the government in Afghanistan said that it would do so if the Americans could provide evidence of Mr. Bin Laden's guilt. But what constitutes adequate evidence of an involvement with terrorism, sufficient to arraign someone on trial? Can there, in practice, be the usual norms of assuming someone innocent until proven guilty when fighting terrorism, when lack of democratic accountability in a group means one doesn't know whom to hold responsible? Certainly, the British, in their war against terrorist groups in Northern Ireland, did not wholly keep to the usual norms of liberal law. Hence the prevention of Terrorism Act of 1974 allowed for detention without trial, but even more important the British in Northern Ireland instituted special courts in which it was easier to obtain convictions in terrorist offenses, the so-called Diplock Courts. (These courts acquired this name from the man who set them up, Lord Diplock.) Protection of sources of information in the hands of the security forces was undoubtedly one reason at least for the decreased form of accountability and transparency in the operation of these courts. Again, what constitutes evidence for someone to face a charge of terrorism? Would the sort of standards of the Diplock Courts be acceptable internationally? Would Afghanistan have assumed that Mr. Bin Laden would have received a fair trial under some American equivalent?

Certainly, one can ask how safe were the convictions within the Diplock Courts and in that regard observe that when in 1999 most of those convicted by those courts in Northern Ireland were let out under license provided they didn't again engage in terrorism, there seems to have been little doubt that the great majority had indeed been involved in terrorism. Not every detail of their convictions might have been wholly correct but the overwhelming majority seem to have been guilty enough to have been justifiably locked up.

One problem raised by all this is the challenge to traditions of "hospitality" which a state may grant someone thought to be kin in some way. Thus, there was the interesting case of "hospitality" extended by Saudi Arabia to the Muslim Idi Amin, the former dictator of the East African state of Uganda from 1971 to 1979, who had engaged in appalling slaughters of innocent people whilst dictator. Indeed, I seem to recall that Amin personally assassinated a Christian priest, Bishop Luwwum, publicly on television. But Amin was never handed over to the international police, although he had not been a Saudi by birth, and he was given shelter by the Saudis after 1979. Various other ex-dictators have lived out their last years protected by one or other state from being brought to justice, and questions of hospitality apply in these cases too. It was "hospitality" that Afghanistan extended to Bin Laden.

So much for some thoughts about terrorism and the legal system. Ultimately, it seems to me that there is only so much the legal system can do to contain the maiming and killing by groups of private individuals. Thus, one vital ingredient in fighting terrorism seems to me to be the development of traditions of democracy and of politics. Thus the Irish Republican Army is just that—an army to which a political organization, namely Sinn Fein, is tacked on. This is why the IRA has found decommissioning of its weapons so difficult—who ever heard of an army destroying its weapons without admitting that it had been beaten? In which case was decommissioning of weapons an admission of defeat? It has proved extremely difficult to introduce a political level of reality, as distinct from a military one, into this debate.

By contrast, the African National Congress of South Africa was in its fight against apartheid, a political organization through and through, and after 1960 it developed an armed wing. But politics was in control, and attempts to brand the ANC a terrorist organization were extremely inept. It engaged in only a tiny number of attacks against white civilians despite the immense provocation of the existence of apartheid for decade after decade. The fact of the ANC's political level surely has had much to do with the obvious superiority of the level of democracy in post-apartheid South Africa, as compared to what has issued in the West Bank and Gaza Strip from the Palestine National Council.

There is in all this an interesting failure to observe a fundamental fact about democracy, and that is that democracy is, in one sense, the most authoritarian form of government that there is. Without going as far as Mao Zedong, who used to talk of democracy as the People's Democratic Dictatorship, the fact is that democracy is a process whereby an individual or a party gets a mandate from the majority of those who bother to vote to carry out certain policies, and no-one else has such a mandate. Here is a fundamental asymmetry, and it makes democracy one of the most authoritarian forms of government. This can be vital to containing terrorism; thus, for example, although David Ben Gurion, Israel's first prime minister, did not put terrorists like Menachem Begin and Yitzchak Shamir on trial for their terrorist offenses, Ben Gurion did triumph over them politically. Begin and Shamir were forced after 1948 to work within what Israeli democracy permitted them.

A good example of what an absence of liberal democracy in such circumstances can make for was the circulation within the Muslim countries after September 11th of the story that the Israeli secret service had been responsible for the attacks of September 11th, and that some four thousand Jews had stayed away from work at the World Trade Center on September 11th, after being tipped off. The fact that no details of these alleged four thousand has been

163

produced, names, addresses, firms for whom they worked, where they are now working, etc, should alert any student of symmetrization that this allegation is in the realm of something discussed in chapter 6 of this book, namely abstract abstraction. The operation of this abstraction is only further aided when one reflects on the fact that all the attackers of September 11th were Muslim Arabs who came from outside Israel. By contrast, the dubious claim that Zionists used to make, that the Arabs who left Israel in 1948 did so voluntarily, in response to radio broadcasts instructing them to do so, is now seldom repeated because it has been possible in the open democratic situation in Israel to point to the lack of evidence for this claim: as I noted earlier no recordings of these alleged broadcasts have ever been produced, which were the radio stations broadcasting these alleged messages, on what frequencies did they broadcast, how many Arabs had radios in 1948, why are there no reference to these alleged broadcasts in any Arab newspapers of the day, etc. The lack of democratic openness in most Arab states on September 11th has meant that the story of Israeli complicity in the attacks of that day have yet to be refuted, and months later the story was still being recycled.

In this regard, it may be that the battle of terrorism may at some point require democracy to confront the fact that none of the various Holy Books of the Jews, Christians and Muslims show much commitment to democracy. They tend instead to imply, so it seems to me, that God is not a parliament. But then it is only in countries which have been liberal democracies for several generations that there is toleration of open critical refutation in public of the dubious claims, especially the dubious moral claims contained in Holy Books. After all, the very first verse of the Qur'an, Sura 2, verse 1, is rendered into English by Mr. Dawood as: "This book is not to be doubted."

16

Democracy and the Future after September 11th

This last chapter is an attempt to bring together the ideas of the previous chapters so as to try and integrate them into a coherent position. The first and most basic point is that although soldiers and police have some role to play in the struggle against terrorism, at the end of the day this struggle can only be won at the political level of reality. This book has therefore been my attempt to stay at this level of reality, for it is the failure to do this which is the biggest problem of bringing this struggle to a successful conclusion, and at the earliest possible date.

To see where the argument has got to so far, I will briefly summarize it. We began by noting that the attackers of September 11th acted from motives that they would have derived from their religion, and a striking feature of religion is that it deals with the infinite. Thus, the belief that one is acting to defend one's religion makes it easy to believe that whatever one does to defend it is infinitely justified. This can be a great license for terrorism.

The early chapters showed that it is possible to produce perceptions of infinity by means of a process called symmetrization and in this way it becomes possible to explain many dubious infinities, such as the beliefs of the depressive of their infinite worthlessness, such as the belief that God is infinitely powerful, infinitely knowing and infinitely just or loving, the infinities of heaven and hell and those postulated by the Nazis in which Aryanism became a collection of sublime infinities whilst Jewishness became an infinity of degradation and filth. Karl Marx's loathing of capitalism as a whole, despite his lyrical praise of it in the Communist Manifesto of 1848, was argued to derive in a similar way. This, in turn, raised the question as to whether anything could be done about such pathological symmetrization in respect of public life and it was argued that liberal democracy is that form of society where those infinities that had been produced by one or other symmetrization were most likely to be exposed, and their nature as inauthentic infinities made clear. Also, whilst there have been forms of politics between states for several thousand years, liberal democracy was also that form of polity in which politics could actually operate within a state. From these two considerations, it followed that liberal democracy was not just one form of government amongst many other equally valid forms, nor just one point of view, but rather that liberal democracy enjoys a justly privileged position. Within a liberal democracy, the citizens have some chance to actually attain the political level of reality itself, experience it, and are most likely to think in terms of political accommodation with others. Terrorism is, by contrast, an attempt to short-circuit the political level of reality, and to pretend (with the Irish Republican Army) that earthly power "flows from the barrel of a gun."

Meanwhile, if it is infinity that is seductive, and if liberal democracy is that kind of polity that is most destructive of fantasized, inauthentic infinities, such as the attributes of God, then liberal democracy is bound to seem colorless and dull to many people, and this would make the demise of such infinities very difficult and slow. The great slowness in the demise of revealed religion seems a likely example of this. Religious militants of all kinds find it all too easy to perceive liberal democracy to be spiritually empty, and this would function for them as a definite legitimation of, and encouragement to, terrorism against it.

At this point, the argument was widened. It needed to be because to imagine that dubious infinities can be de-infinitized and given up merely as a result of intellectual argument is an old fantasy of eighteenth century French rationalism. For large minorities of a people to broadly discard dubious infinities, such as those found in religion, that do so much to power terrorism, it is necessary that a large part of that people cease to live in dire poverty, and this raised the question of economics, or to call it by its proper political name, political economy. On the day of the attacks in New York and Washington, the world's political economy included such things as rapid urbanization in many countries in a context of globalization and of the World Trade Organization. Since the attackers of September 11th were presumably opposed to liberal capitalism as a system, it was firstly necessary to examine whether this made a vital contribution to the well-being of humanity. Chapter 11 argues that it does make a vital contribution, and that the contribution of the United States is especially great. However, the system of liberal capitalism is also subject to long waves of growth, such as that which occurred between 1948 and 1973 when economic growth was generally good and reliable, but which was then followed by the period between 1973 and the mid 1990s when growth was much less likely and unreliable. It was argued that another such period of poor and generally unreliable growth is due to return between 2015–2020, and that in our present circumstances of rapid urbanization, such a long-term slowdown would be a massive disaster and a large encouragement to terrorism. However, it was also argued that the negative features of such a period are now avoidable for the first time in history, and could be prevented by accelerating research into renewable energy. Success at greatly bringing down the price of renewable energy would help the world economy to grow, and would enable the governments of the urbanizing countries to greatly improve matters in their rural areas, and thus slow down urbanization, thus reducing the large shock that urbanization initially produces. The trauma of mass urbanization in England was memorably explored by E.P.

Thompson in *The Making of the English Working Class,* Penguin, London 1981.

It is the depth of the shock of urbanization which seems to me to provide the context for terrorism, although for terrorism to occur requires numerous other ingredients as well. But people who have grown up in a country which is predominantly urbanized, such as Britain or the United States, probably have difficulty in imagining the disorientation that being first generation in a modern urban context tends to afford. Not merely do many first time urban dwellers lack the skills to secure their next meal, but this economic insecurity attunes with a new insecurity of identity, which now experiences the general disregard for traditional authority, whether by the open questioning of the beliefs of religion, shocking encounters with feminism, with the open expression of homosexuality or with the inescapable discovery that one's own people have no magic immunity from the operation within it of incest and child abuse along with forms of intervention by foreign powers, whether economic or military. Complex and shifting mixtures of all these things can power an appalled reaction on the part of some people to all these and does something to produce the rage and fury of religious militants, such as those from within Judaism, Christianity, Islam and Hinduism. For this reason, there is no single cause of terrorism, and therefore no one single thing to do about it, but the arguments of the foregoing suggest the vital need firstly for liberal democracy and secondly for the most economically advanced liberal democracies to minimize long-term economic slowdown.

I will illustrate the above ideas with a case study, namely the struggle against apartheid, and now as an old veteran of this struggle, some things are clearer to me than they were during the struggle. At first sight, apartheid has nothing to do with political Islam, because political Islam is by intention non-racial, whereas apartheid was racialist through and through. But although there is indeed this difference, to assume that there is only this difference between political Islam and apartheid would be to make the mistake of symmetrization. Thus, I note that the apartheid thinkers did not invent the domination of black people in South Africa by white people; it had been like this for nearly three centuries before 1948 when the apartheid government took power. Before this time, although black people had protested their repression, they had had no means to be at all effective in their protests. However, South Africa's participation in World War II (on the anti-Nazi side) changed all that, because as a result South Africa's capitalist, commodity-producing economy grew very fast and unprecedented numbers of white and black people urbanized. It was this new urban existence that for the first time really allowed black people to challenge their oppression through strikes and political campaigns of all kinds. Apartheid was the enraged, shocked reaction of whites, especially by whites who had themselves recently moved to the cities, to the new challenges to white racial domination which they had hitherto taken for granted as being God given. As I've earlier argued, a considerable part of political Islam is also the attempt to reassert what had been tacitly taken for granted—again as God given—but which is now under challenge in such places as the Middle East, North Africa, and in parts of Asia as a result of urbanization in a world order dominated economically and politically by liberal capitalism and by norms of individual choice. Therefore, we can learn some lessons from the struggle against apartheid, namely that its success eventually became a worldwide struggle waged mainly at the political level. There was on occasion some small role for soldiers and security forces in that struggle, but mainly it was a political struggle and the victory of the African National Congress led by Nelson Mandela was a political victory. Of course, not all of the details of the struggle against apartheid need be exactly relevant in our post September 11th situation: thus, the chief economic tactic of economically isolating apartheid via economic sanctions probably has much less relevance in the new situation. This example again illustrates how between any two situations differences exist in a context of their similarities, and their similarities exist in a context of their differences. The mistake—or the evasive sub-honesty—is to try and separate these out, and to pretend that it is all one or the other. That, at any rate, is part of the wisdom that one is encouraged to embrace by the idea of symmetrization.

I have spoken several times of the "political level or reality" and I have done so for the following reason. When someone explains something, for example explains heat as due to the vibration of molecules, this is a kind of reductionism, because the experience of heat is intellectually reduced to something else, the vibration. Such a reduction is what might be called reductionism of a "good" kind. By contrast, if I try to explain say child abuse as something which occurs because someone has faulty genes, then this is almost certainly entirely false, and involves reducing something that is social and psychological—child abuse—to something that is biological, namely genes. This is reductionism of a "bad" kind. Of course, child-abusers have genes like everyone else but what has happened here is that in attempting to invoke the genetic level of reality some vital psychological attributes of child abusers have been lost, or symmetrized out. That is to say, reductionism of a bad kind is the result of a whole-part symmetrization. Whole-part symmetrization is also exactly what happens when people reduce the political level of reality to something else, such as the barrel of a gun. The felt infinity they thereby acquire is a moral infinity, such as feeling that the (terrorist) behavior that derives from this has infinite and unquestionable justification. Once again, symmetrization results from abstract abstraction. It is against the operation of such reductionist symmetrization that the operation of the norms of liberal democracy sometimes offer some protection.

Democracy versus Terrorism

I have claimed that the operation of liberal democracy is vital to combat terrorism but I have yet to have any discussion as to what democracy is. Others have argued democracy is about hierarchies of competence and I agree with this. For example, in the dying days of the presidency of George Bush Sr. in 1992, the United States signed up to the North American Free Trade Agreement, NAFTA. To pretend that the idea of NAFTA came unbidden from the American people is plainly false. The chances are that not one American in a hundred has ever read just what their government signed the American people up to when this Agreement was eventually ratified by the U.S. Senate. That is where democracy as hierarchies of competence comes in. To expect the average voter to have read such an agreement, and to have understood its sometimes technical legalistic language, is entirely unrealistic. The American electorate has some sort of trust in its legislators, and assumes that these will broadly act in the interests of the American people as a whole. Given the resources of understanding required to form a knowledgeable opinion on just a single question, democratic electorates have no choice but to trust the legislators who got the most votes to do their best. At least their choices may be criticized in public, and this, in turn, in the best circumstances allows people to experience the sheer difficulty and complexity of any process of political accommodation. Such are the practical limits on Abraham Lincoln's definition of democracy in his Gettysburg Address as "government by the people for the people and of the people." In Israeli democracy, the system of proportional representation usually results in parliaments where up to ten political parties are represented. As a result, all Israeli governments have been coalitions, sometimes of numerous parties. Certainly, the failure of Israeli democracy to sustain Ehud Barak as prime minister for a full four or five year period when he was slowly feeling his way towards a political accommodation with the Palestinians in 2000 and 2001 was a great failure of Israeli democracy. It was Israel's most culpable contribution to the political impasse which was so evidently the situation on the day of the attacks in New York and Washington. A rule which required a political party to obtain at least 5 percent of the vote before obtaining representation in parliament is one, at least, of the changes needed. Here is one example of how the institutions of democracy badly need strengthening in our post-September 11th situation.

The Maintenance and Extension of Democracy

If I am right to think that it is the strong stable operation of democracy that is the best way to attack the development of terrorism, because then maximum proportions of the population can attain the political level of reality, then this raises at least two questions. Firstly, how can this type of polity be extended to the rest of the world that doesn't yet have it, and secondly, how can those countries that have democratic functioning be strengthened to fight off attempts by religious and other militants to overthrow or manipulate them?

So far as the first question goes, we have to ask what is likely to make liberal democracy attractive to those who don't have it? It seems to be universal that all peoples wish to be respected; one major way to be respected is to make creative advances which will be appreciated across cultural barriers. Creative contributions to mathematics and the natural sciences are obvious examples of this. The creative center of humanity one thousand years before the attacks of September 11th was the Muslim Middle East and this fact has led some Islamic militants to claim that Islam is compatible with the much more rapid creativity of our own time, but this much greater creative pace makes this utterly unlikely. Certainly if, as I assume, there are no biological impediments which would reduce any people's chances of making creative contributions, then every people is potentially capable of making a creative contribution to all manner of disciplines, scientific, artistic, etc. Thus algebra, it seems to me, was not invented by any one people but is rather a magnificent example of what non-racial cooperation of dozens of peoples and cultures can achieve. Such contributions are most likely to be greatest in conditions of democratic openness as this is the social atmosphere that most encourages creativity. This theory is supported by the fact that whereas Germany, before the Nazis, had been a center of world science, philosophy, music and mathematics, the Nazi period was one of the least creative in recent German history. The Soviet countries were also strikingly uncreative and for similar reasons: conformity was what was expected of the citizen, not criticism, without which creativity receives much less encouragement. My conclusion is that respect that comes from a level of creativity that might get a people noticed is most likely in liberal democratic conditions. It is necessary to value creativity at least as highly as conformity to moral norms is now valued, such as the norms thought to derive from holy books. This leads to a fundamental alteration in world outlook. If this were applied to a worldwide education of biology, as I advocated in chapter 14, it could lead to decreases in human suffering, and lessen the vast waste of resources where people miss work due to illness. If participated in by tens of thousands of scientists of all races and creeds from across the world, it could be another wonderful example of what anti-racialist liberal capitalism could amount to in practice.

This still leaves the old problem of liberal democracy: does one allow those who would destroy democracy to use the openness of democracy to do just that, as the Weimar Republic allowed the Nazi Party to do, between 1930 and 1933? No. I think we should learn from this lesson. If terrorism can only be defeated politically, and if that means the operation of liberal democracy, but this has to be suspended by the army (as was done in Algeria in 1992) then where are we in the democratizing anti-terrorist stakes? I think that the answer is that there is not just one negation of liberal democracy, the way there is only one operation of negation in formal logic, in which every sentence is either true or false. I think that there are numerous negations of democracy; apartheid was one, but as I argued in chapter 10, one of the less bad things about political life under apartheid was that it was always possible and in public to cut politicians and government generally down to size. Inauthentic infinities, e.g. involving a cult of personality such as that which tended to surround the architect of apartheid, Dr. Verwoerd, were thereby kept under some sort of control. This is vital. By contrast, the Shah of Iran, by building a laughable cult of invincibility about himself, helped strengthen the mode of thinking which helped the Iranian Revolution of 1979 to occur. One crucial thing is that it must be possible to publicly de-infinitize inauthentic infinities surrounding public life, and public figures in their public capacities, otherwise the psychological ground for the dubious infinities of religious or fascist militants is being prepared. Although apartheid's racial criterion of who had the vote is wholly unacceptable, perhaps since the attacks in New York and Washington is it possible that a qualified franchise based on money or property is the least bad thing that could be done in the direction of democracy in some of the urbanizing countries? Such a policy would plainly be elitist, but then as I have argued, democracy is in any case about hierarchies of competence. I suggest that if I'm correct about the vital necessity of democracy to allow as many as people as possible to think in terms of the political level of reality, then perhaps a non-racial, non-sexist property-based franchise would be preferable to rule by the army and preferable to one party rule or rule by any male or female dictator without exception.

It is this whole idea that one party or one person possesses enough virtue or knowledge or wisdom that is, in conditions of modern complexity, the major ignorant fairy-tale and this is something which needs to be established in the culture(s) of a country

174

for liberal democracy to become viable. The attainment of such a level of political culture would be a central task of the period of qualified franchise. Of course, such a policy could only get legitimacy if the governments that resulted from such a policy worked hard to finance education and other mechanisms of social development and social mobility. However, if a state adopts such a system this would tend to alienate many who didn't have the vote from that state, and this would undoubtedly play into hands of political Islam which also objects to many of the states left behind in the Middle East by various colonialists from the past. It was probably four centuries of Muslim Ottoman imperialism which has done most to inhibit the development of democracy amongst the Arabs, and amongst the Turks as well. Establishing democracy, or re-establishing it where it has been extinguished, can be one of the most difficult projects imaginable, and the sheer difficulty of the task shows how our social disciplines such as economics, psychology, sociology and anthropology are very far from being sciences, despite the euphemistic use of this term in respect of these disciplines. The development of genuine sciences of intentionality is probably decades away. It requires not more data, of which we have already far too much, but conceptual advance, probably in some ways like the transition from alchemy to modern chemistry.

Certainly, in the circumstances that prevailed on the day of the attacks in New York and Washington there remains the possibility that democracy cannot flourish without considerable economic resources at least. It seems clear that liberal democracy can only function where there is a sizeable middle class, where local or regional loyalties are not too strong and militant, where there are reliable countrywide means of communication so that the whole country really can function as one country, and so on. But is this process of economic development, necessary for a working democracy, always helped by the operation of the World Trade Organization and by globalization? If it is we might ask why it was that America, that now lectures the world on the necessity for the maximum free trade, was for some 160 years between 1787 to 1947 strongly and generally *increasingly* protectionist? After all, America could have chosen instead to have joined Great Britain which between 1847 to 1914 was both the world's biggest trading nation and the staunchest upholder of free trade. Perhaps it wouldn't have been in the interest of protecting the growth and maturing of America's own infant industries to have done so, but in that case, why is it in everyone's self-interest since 1947 to always support all reductions in trade barriers? America certainly owes the world an explanation, and in our post September 11th situation such an explanation acquires increased importance. One thing that evidently powers much of the terrorism is the feeling by religious militants that the heartland of their religion, such as the dar al Islam or home of Islam, is increasingly penetrated by America. Is this political economic penetration in *all* its forms, *always* in the best interests of *all* of the peoples of the urbanizing countries, or is this belief just another whole-part symmetrization, this time within liberal capitalist political economy?

There was on the day of the attacks in New York and Washington on September 11th 2001 a World Trade Organization, but there was no World Prosperity to Spread Democracy Organization. Are these two things the same? I have implicitly argued that the example of the United States itself suggests that "it ain't necessarily so!" But I have yet to see the experience of America in this matter being used in studies of why some trade barriers may well be worth retaining, at least for a time. Surely, too, there should be university professorships within departments of economics to study long-term unreliable growth periods or professorships in slump studies? This is especially so given the tendency when one is in the phase of reliable growth of the long wave to think that this reliable growth part of the long wave is the whole, that is to engage in symmetrization. That symmetrization was the assumption of middle-class life, especially in the United States of the 1920s and of the 1950s and 1960s, and during the 1990s the form taken by this make-believe was of supposedly automatic permanent economic growth via the brave new world of consumer electronics, the so-called "New Economy" which was supposed to make for a "Goldilocks Economy." Yet a long-term recession or a slump are amongst the gravest events that can occur in the whole realm of political economy and the period of unreliable growth that is due to begin between 2015 and 2020 could have especially severe political economic consequences in our post-September 11th world if we don't apply some foresight.

All this is, of course, very much within liberal capitalism, but it is a liberal capitalist political economy which has some new extra foresight built into it. Perhaps the sort of project argued for in this book should be called the project of foresight capitalism?

Bibliography

Causes and Consequences of the Great Depression, Stewart Ross, Evans, London 1995.

Coming Plague, The, Laurie Garrett, Penguin, 1994.

Encyclopaedia of the Third Reich, Louis J. Snyder, Wordsworth Editions, 1998.

Globalization in Question, Paul Hirst and Grahame Thompson, Polity Press.

In the Name of Apartheid, Martin Meredith, Hamish Hamilton, London, 1988.

Koran, with Parallel Arabic Text, The, N. J. Dawood, Penguin Classics, 1998.

Leninism, Joseph Stalin, Lawrence and Wishart, London, 1944.

Limits of Liberty, American History 1607–1992, The, Maldwyn A. Jones, Oxford University Press, 1996.

Long Waves of Capitalist Development, The Marshall Lectures given in University of Cambridge, Ernest Mandel, Revised Edition, Verso 1995.

Long Wave Theory, Christopher Freeman (ed.), Edward Elgar, Cheltenham, UK, 1996.

Making of the English Working Class, The, E.P. Thompson, Penguin, 1981.

Middle East Media Research Institute (MEMRI) www.memri.org.

One World Divisible, A Global History since 1945, David Reynolds, Penguin, 2000.

Scientists Against Time, James Phinney Baxter III, MIT Press, 1968.

Semites and Anti-Semites, Bernard Lewis, London, 1997.

Skeptical Environmentalist, The, Bjorn Lomborg, Cambridge University Press, 2001.

Social History of the Third Reich, A, Richard Grunberger, Penguin, 1974.

Theories of Surplus Value, Karl Marx, Progress Publishers, Moscow, 1968, Volume 2.

Timeless Energy of the Sun, The, UNESCO World Solar Program, Madanjeet Singh, Thames and Hudson, 1998.

Unconscious as Infinite Sets, The, I. Matte Blanco, Duckworth, London, 1975.